TOWARDS 2000

THE FUTURE
OF POST-SECONDARY
EDUCATION IN ONTARIO

From the Report prepared for the Committee of Presidents of Universities of Ontario by its Subcommittee on Research and Planning presented as a brief to the Commission on Post-Secondary Education in Ontario

with a foreword by
Claude Bissell

MCCLELLAND AND STEWART LIMITED

0-7710-0149-5 (cloth)
0-7710-0150-9 (paper)

The Canadian Publishers
McClelland and Stewart Limited
25 Hollinger Road, Toronto 374

PRINTED AND BOUND IN CANADA BY
WEB OFFSET PUBLICATIONS LTD.

The Subcommittee is composed of the following

John Porter   *Pauline Jewett*
Bernard Blishen *John B. Macdonald*
John R. Evans   *Robin Ross*
Bertrand L. Hansen *Bernard Trotter*
Robin S. Harris *Ross B. Willis*
Frances Ireland

TABLE OF CONTENTS

FOREWORD   xi

1 Post-Secondary Education in the Emerging Context of
  Post-Industrialism   1

  *Characteristics of the post-industrial society–role of hu-
  manists and of social scientists–educational requirements–
  –a developing national culture dependent upon expanded
  educational resources–individual and institutional freedom*

2 The March of Events   11

  Universities   12
  Teachers Colleges   14
  Colleges of Applied Arts and Technology   16
  Ryerson Polytechnical Institute   18
  Colleges of Agricultural Technology   18
  Schools of Nursing   19
  Other Professional Schools   19
  The Significant Trends since 1965   19
  Present Institutional Structures and Interrelations   21

3 The Alteration of Roles   25

  The Professors of the Future   29
  Tenure and Collective Bargaining   33
  The Students of the Future   38

4 The Power of Numbers   47

  *The Development of the Ontario University System
  in the 1960's*   48
  Anticipated Patterns of Enrolment Growth in the 1970's   49
  *Projected Enrolments in Non-University
  Post-Secondary Institutions*   56
  *Post-Secondary Enrolment and Participation
  Rates in 1980*   58

5 The Model of Accessible Hierarchy 61

The "Conscription" Issue 65
The Institutional Base 66
The Model of Accessible Hierarchy:
A New Role for the Colleges 69
Old and New Roles for the Universities 70
Ryerson Polytechnical Institute 71
Upper Level Accessibility 71

6 The Accessible Baccalaureate 73

Centrality of "generalist" education–need for multiple access–alternatives examined–a systems approach to the teaching/learning process

7 The Professional Ladder 81

Respective Roles of Colleges and Universities 83
Duration of Professional Education 87
Continuing Education and Requalification 89
Influence of Professional Associations 90
Manpower Production and the Proliferation of Professions 92

8 The Highest Learning 95

Development of program appraisal and discipline assessment in Ontario universities–long-term factors as a guide to development of graduate programs–an "open-door" policy–the problem of over-specialization–a restructured Ph.D. program–research in relation to the training of graduate students

9 The Extension of Knowledge 106

Financial Support of Research 107
Science Policy for Canada 113
The Goals of University Research 115
The Federal Role in the Support of Research 121
The Division of Costs 121

10 The Federal Role   123

Post-secondary education the concern of both federal and provincial governments–a divided responsibility–areas of federal responsibility to date–continuing and expanding the federal presence in post-secondary education–proposed federal spending in post-secondary sectors to relate to national needs and objectives–a distinct minister and department required.

11 The Allocation of Costs   138

Financial Assistance to Students   146
Provincial Revenues and Expenditures on Education   152
Projected Costs to Government   158

12 The Interface with Government   163

Mechanisms for handling relations between government and universities–integrated department for post-secondary education–integrated advisory group–regional considerations

EPILOGUE   168

REFERENCES   173

FOREWORD
by
Claude Bissell

The most remarkable characteristic of the Ontario system of higher education is that it has been largely fashioned by the universities themselves. Despite its constitutional responsibility for higher education, Ontario, like all the other Canadian provinces, had, until the early sixties, given little sustained attention to the university problem. Support to universities was on no fixed basis, and was often determined casually by informal arrangements. Any long-range planning among universities tended to have a federal bias, because it was the federal government that had rescued the universities from imminent financial disaster in the post-war years. But, by the early sixties, the Ontario government had become acutely aware that the problem of university development was a major provincial responsibility, and there was a compelling need of a chart for the future.

In the absence of any provincial facility, the task of planning was handed to the universities. This was not entirely an act forced upon the province by its own shortcomings. It was also an indication of the good feeling in general that existed between the province and the universities, and the public faith in the integrity and good sense of the university community. The Committee of Presidents of Universities of Ontario, which comprised all of the central organizational structure, asked a special committee to take on the task of planning for the future. This committee was drawn from the full-time staff, both academic and administrative, of the universities, and it was initially under the chairmanship of John Deutsch, at that time Vice-Principal of Queen's. That committee worked quickly, and drew up the guidelines for expansion during the sixties. It placed particular emphasis on the necessity to expand graduate schools in order to meet the needs for new faculty; and the province responded quickly and magnanimously. This initial committee developed into a Research Committee to which was given continuing responsibility for analyzing basic planning problems that arose from time to time. It was this Committee, for instance, that delineated the nature and function of the

Colleges of Applied Arts and Technology, and first emphasized the possibility of using television to extend the reach of the universities.

The composition and chairmanship of the Research Committee has changed from time to time, but it has retained a central core of members, and a pervasive and self-confident *élan*. Its work has been done largely during weekends and holidays, and from the hours squeezed out of crowded, full-time schedules. The work has been done, too, without remuneration – an example of the disinterested concern so widespread in the University that it is usually ignored by vocal critics. The present study – the largest and most comprehensive of all the studies done by the Research Committee – has been completed without the circumjacent splendours of the government commission – research officers, task forces, transoceanic travel – and, of course, without the conspicuous expenditure of public funds. The report has not suffered from this severe and puritanical approach towards its preparation. Indeed, it has thereby avoided the flatulence of most commission reports; it is clearly and directly written, and moves surely and persuasively to its conclusion.

The report has been produced by the Research Committee under the chairmanship of John Porter. It is a composite work, and it will be easy to distinguish different styles in different chapters. But the general argument was shaped in discussions of the whole Committee, and each chapter was carefully revised and related to the whole. It begins with a statement that sets out the nature of social developments in the next thirty years, and then attempts in subsequent sections to relate specific recommendations to the theoretical assumptions. Theory is constantly reinforced by facts – by analysis of what has happened, and what is likely to happen. The quantitative and the qualitative always move together, but it is the latter that determines the nature of the argument.

The report might be described as an exercise in informed prediction – what must be done, given the nature and needs of society, and the size of the problem. The major virtue of the report is that it jerks us out of our somnolent fixation on the immediate – the Ph.D. glut, student discontent, the Americanization of universities, and the sudden rise in operating costs in universities. It makes us look at long-term trends; it releases us from parochial paralysis; and it challenges our satisfaction with the cracker-barrel philosophy that warms our small-town, provincial hearts.

This is not a report that the academic world will warmly embrace, for it is less than respectful of some of the household gods, and it is quick to acknowledge shortcomings and errors in the academic community. The report does not hesitate to modify some of the earlier ideas of the Research Committee, particularly the role of the CAATs in the developing scheme of higher education.

This report was designed as a submission to the Commission on Post-Secondary Education in Ontario. It will, thus, be one of many submissions, and it will not necessarily carry the easy authority of earlier reports from the Committee of Presidents of Universities of Ontario. The province has now developed its own central planning agency, and the university situation is far more complex than it was four or five years ago. But, whatever effect this report may have on the findings of the Commission, I believe that it will remain as a crucial document in the history of higher education in Canada. I predict it will be widely quoted, praised, criticized, and reviled, and that it will be read and pondered when most of the thousands of pages recently devoted to higher education have mercifully fluttered into oblivion.

CHAPTER 1

POST-SECONDARY EDUCATION
IN
THE EMERGING CONTEXT
OF
POST-INDUSTRIALISM

Post-secondary institutions must be developed in the light of the social changes now taking place and likely to accelerate over the remainder of the twentieth century. Lead time in establishing educational institutions is long. Therefore any decisions involving major changes that are arrived at in the early 1970's are not likely to be implemented for several years and probably will not be "operational" until the late 1970's. Certainly any suggestions about the 1980's will have their effects on those who will live and have a good proportion of their working lives through and beyond the year 2000.

Because it is a dramatic milestone in human chronology, the year 2000 is now attracting a good deal of speculative attention. There are many serious futurologists attempting to outline the main characteristics of the society and of the world of the future – a world in which a good number of the most advanced societies will be brought into increasingly extensive linkages with one another.

These visions of the future vary in the characteristics which they emphasize as being most salient, but they tend to agree on a term to describe the future and on its cultural base. The term is *the post-industrial society,* and its cultural base is supplied by science and technology. There are other names for the future society: the cybernetic society, the service society, and so forth. Its coming is viewed by many with apprehension because of what are believed to be its inevitable dehumanizing qualities, but it has, if its capacities are properly used, a great potential to improve human life. Many of the major aims of social reform – improving the standard of living and the quality of life of many, giving aid to the underdeveloped world, and most of the other concerns of our age – can only be achieved by the application of scientific and technological resources, and post-industrialism does have this potential.

The beginnings of the post-industrial society are already with us, and can be analyzed. According to Daniel Bell, who has written much about it, there are five main characteristics.[1] The first is the creation of a service economy, with the majority of the labour force producing services rather than goods. This condition is simply a continuation of the expansion of the tertiary level occupations that we have been experiencing. Herman Kahn suggests[2] that a quaternary level of occupations is developing, rendering services "to tertiary occupations or to each other."

Bell's second criterion is what he calls the preeminence of the professional and technical class. These are the rapidly expanding occupations, and the workers in them are the symbol of post-industrialism as the semi-skilled worker was the symbol of the industrial period.

The third characteristic is the centrality of theoretical knowledge. It has long been said that knowledge is power; for post-industrialism it is theoretical and abstract knowledge which is the basis of innovative power. Thus the post-industrial society is organized around knowledge.

---

[1]Daniel Bell, "Notes on the Post-Industrial Society," *The Public Interest*, Winter 1967, and Spring, 1967; and "The Measurement of Knowledge and Technology," in E.B. Sheldon and W.E. Moore, *Indicators of Social Change* (New York: Russell Sage, 1968), pp. 145 ff.
[2]Herman Kahn and Anthony J. Wiener, *The Year 2000* (New York: Macmillan, 1967), p. 63.

Fourthly, this society has a commitment to growth and innovation, which gives rise to the need for planning and forecasting and controlling the advance of technological change.

Finally, there is the creation of the new intellectual technology of linear programming, systems analysis, information theory, all of which are important in the macro-analysis of masses of data. Decision-making must increasingly have such a technological base.

Because knowledge is central to the post-industrial society, the dominant figures which are emerging are the scientists, the engineers, the mathematicians, the economists, the creators and the consumers of the computer technology. These stand in contrast to the dominant men of the industrial period – the entrepreneur, the business man and the industrial executive. Consequently, Bell says, "the dominant institutions of the new society will be the intellectual institutions. The leadership of the new society will rest, not with businessmen or corporations as we know them . . . but with the research corporation, the industrial laboratories, the experimental stations and the universities."[3] He continues:

> If the business firm was the key institution of the past one hundred years, because of its role in organizing production for the mass creation of products, the university will become the central institution of the next hundred years because of its role as the new source of innovation and knowledge.[4]

A further feature of the post-industrial society which it is important to note is the greatly increased role of government in exploiting the potential of post-industrialism and the establishing of provincial and national goals. Most of the great planning problems left by the industrial period – urbanization, pollution, common standards of social rights which are increasingly a part of the rising expectations of the less privileged sectors of the society – will be solved in the post-industrial era through

---

[3] Daniel Bell, "Notes on the Post-Industrial Society," *The Public Interest,* Winter, 1967, p. 27.
[4] *Ibid.,* p. 30.

3

the political system rather than by market forces which
throughout the industrial period were sanctified as the grea
regulator of human welfare. The political system will see grea
debates about alternative futures, but whatever the choices they
will be collectively pursued through public policy although not
necessarily by public agencies. Consequently there will be a
great reduction of the importance of the concept of profit.
Already the rapidly expanding sectors of the economy are the
non-industrial ones, and this is likely to continue as governments at all levels assume greater responsibilities in the planning and direction of social change.

A more familiar and less optimistic view of the emerging
society is provided by John Kenneth Galbraith in *The New
Industrial State*. However, like Bell, Galbraith emphasizes the
importance of trained intelligence and gives a central role to
educational and research institutions. "They stand," he says,
"in relation to the industrial system, much as did the banking
and financial community to the earlier stages of industrial development."[5]

Because the culture of the future will be based on science and
technology and because experts trained in these areas will
play key roles, it will be more essential than ever to strengthen
the traditional disciplines which concern themselves with moral
and aesthetic values. The value choices which become available
with a greatly expanded scientific capacity are more numerous
and more difficult to make. New discoveries in the biological
sciences, in genetics for example, illustrate the moral questions
we will be facing in the future. There will also be the competing
claims of the various sciences for their own particular development, requiring decisions about the social role of science that
are beyond the competence of scientists *qua* scientists to make.[6]
Thus the humanists must ensure (to use the jargon) that the
insights and principles derived from their "proper study" are

---

[5]J. K. Galbraith, *The New Industrial State* (Boston: Houghton Mifflin, 1967),
p. 282.
[6]We have found some of the papers in the 1968 Special issue of *Daedalus* very
helpful in drawing up this picture of the anticipated changes over the next
thirty years.

included in the input data system, or they will have no effect on
the system output. They will need to combat the regimentation
that could so easily get out of hand simply for convenience of
computer programming. They will need to reassert the worth of
the individual – of *many*-dimensional man. They will need to
strive toward new forms of beauty in a world where change will
often outpace interpretation, and to find new principles – or
new applications of old principles – of morality in a rapidly
changing and increasingly complex social life. The multi-bil-
lion-person world will be a more crowded one requiring higher
levels of civility; also, perhaps, since it will be a largely urban
world, requiring new forms of social organization which we
must look to the social sciences to develop.

Pre-eminent among the problems facing the social scientists
will be that of designing appropriate governmental institutions.
Though much has been written about the technical and scientific innovations of the post-industrial society, very little has been
said about the future of democracy as it has developed in its
political forms, at least, in many western societies. Is it true as
Galbraith asserts that power will increasingly rest with the
technostructure? Is it not more likely that the technostructure
itself will be taken over by powerful economic or political interests – interests that will be increasingly remote from popular
control and accountability, bypassing representative institutions?[7]

The social control of science and technology for human benefit will no doubt increasingly require government intervention.
Probably there will also be "people" intervention, which we see
already appearing in community-based citizen groups. Such
disciplines as political science and sociology will probably take
over from economics as the significant post-industrial social
sciences, and join with the humanistic disciplines in the eternal
task of defining and establishing the good life in the good
society. For a federated society such as Canada's the task is
even more complex since antiquated levels of government –

---

[7]For a critical note on the problems of power in the post-industrial society see
N. Birnbaum, "Is there a Post-Industrial Revolution?," *Social Policy*, July-
August 1970, Vol. 1, No. 2.

provinces in relation to large metropolitan areas, for example –
may have to be restructured in relation to each other. In working on this task it may be more important than formerly to
protect the institutions of higher learning as the major sources
of moral and social change and as critical appraisers and moni-
tors of the staggering rate of scientific and technical change. At
this time in history one can sense in Canada and beyond a
growing authoritarianism and impatience with dissent. The
safeguards for intellectual freedom must be given the most serious consideration as all our educational systems become dependent on government.

Despite the fact that he is rationalizing his world through
science and technology, man will never be totally rational or
wholly intellectual. In fact, in the world of the future we might
expect an extension of those patterns of behaviour which we
can now see and which arc, in effect, a reaction to over-ration-
alization of life and to impersonal bureaucratic forms of organization. The new culture of science and technology will no
doubt impose an efficiency on many areas of life through the
application of scientific method to the management of social
institutions. Living in a world thus rationalized, people will
seek new forms of escape or adaptation in the search for new
forms of transcendental experience. These experiences will be
sought in a variety of ways: through drugs, through new sexual
morality, through withdrawal to isolated and occult communities. Institutions of higher learning may well have to consider
developing studies of these phenomena, and to search for ways
in which the non-intellectual needs of man can be served. Universities have had their origins in, and until recently have been
closely linked to, the traditional religious denominations. While
there is not likely to be any great religious revival in the traditional sense, there are likely to be increasing movements in
search of new meaning and experience to counter the rationalization of society's major institutions, and, perhaps, to meet a
need of one of the dimensions of many-dimensional man. In
the world of the future, therefore, higher educational needs will
by no means be confined to the production of scientists and
technologists.

Although as we have just said the highly trained human
resources required in the future will run across all intellectual
disciplines, the training of scientists – and here we would in-

6

:lude social scientists and managers as their disciplines become
:ncreasingly based on mathematics – poses particularly difficult
problems for the post-industrial age. As the society and the
knowledge upon which it is based become more complex, it
becomes more difficult for individuals to assimilate the increased amount of complex knowledge that must be acquired.
The possibilities of serious shortages of people who can handle
the greater levels of complexity of knowledge are great. Thus
there must be a very real talent search through all social levels
and groups. This need is a long-term reality which any furore
about unemployed Ph.D.'s should not be permitted to mask.
But the assimilation of knowledge is difficult, and learning is
irksome. Hence, able people must be motivated to study, and
not be lost as a vital social resource because of environments or
circumstances which inhibit their growth. There is no substitute
for hard work, or high quality. Universities have always had
great concern for excellence, for developing the very highest of
human potential. Whatever the system of higher education
this quality of excellence should not be downgraded.

  For many, the notion of excellence has elitist connotations,
and hence they believe it contradicts the ideal of equality which
has quite rightly become one of the most important criteria by
which modern societies are judged. Indeed, educational systems
have been severely criticized for streaming practices which give
special consideration to those who give early evidence of supe-
rior ability, since it is the middle and upper class children
whose abilities become most apparent, while lower in the socio-
economic scale, in sub-cultures less conducive to learning, children cannot so easily demonstrate their abilities. However, it is
wrong to make the same kind of judgements about the social
effects of sorting out excellence at the level of the higher learning, because it is indisputable that human beings are unequal in
terms of the amount of complex knowledge they can assimilate.
A system of higher education must assume or at least argue
strongly for a system of education at the lower levels which
constantly seeks to eliminate, as far as possible, the social effects of poor learning environments. We would visualize, for
Ontario, a highly pluralistic or differentiated post-secondary
system in which many needs and levels of ability would be
served, including some degree of open admissions for particularly deprived groups. Within this differentiated system, howev-

er, there must somewhere be special concern for excellence and for the education of all the good brains that can be mustered.

We have placed great emphasis on the increased role of science and technology in the post-industrial world. There are important consequences of that development which should be considered by those planning post-secondary education. One of these, for example, is the way the world of work becomes changed by the creation of new occupations and specializations. At the same time sets of older occupations become reorganized while others are destroyed altogether. The professional division of labour is likely to proliferate and to become increasingly hierarchical from the most highly trained specialists at the top to the paraprofessional workers at the base. Thus new professional and paraprofessional workers will contribute peculiarly specialized tasks to a co-operating work group, while the solo practising professional is likely to disappear because he cannot possibly acquire himself all the complex knowledge and skill that science has made available to him. Professional self-regulation and monopoly will probably be greatly reduced by the public concern for the adequate delivery of professional services such as law, welfare and medicine. Educational requirements, then, will range from the need for the most highly specialized worker whose training culminates in postgraduate research institutes, on the one hand, to the skills of the technologist and technician whose training is most appropriately provided at the polytechnic or college level, on the other. One effect of this hierarchical structure of professional work and education is that people can become cut off from advancement because their training is limited and they are forever labelled as paraprofessionals. The educational processes of the future should be such that they provide for continuity and the acquisition of higher qualifications. All those on professional teams will be linked together by new applications of computer technology in, for example, medical diagnosis, library retrieval and programmed learning.

The last-mentioned of these computer applications reminds us that new technologies are being and will continue even more to be applied to the educational processes. Many who feel overwhelmed at the increasing costs of post-secondary education look to the new technology to make savings. This may or may not prove to be the case, but there are various new approaches that deserve the most careful consideration by educational planners. What must also be considered is the possibility of improving pedagogical techniques to facilitate the assimilation of knowledge.

Another feature of post-industrialism which educational planners must seriously consider will be the way in which different societies will penetrate and intervene in each other's activities. This will create new needs for trans-national co-operation through new trans-national institutions.[8] It would be possible for any one society to achieve the benefits of the future by becoming absorbed in the more rapid advance of another one – a fate that many Canadians fear as so many of their own institutions become absorbed by or linked with those of the United States, particularly the two most significant carriers of post-industrialism: the modern multi-national corporations and the universities. Perhaps there would be nothing wrong with such absorption if the culture of post-industrialism is homogeneous. One sure mechanism for such absorption is to rely on external recruitment of highly qualified people as an alternative to training them at home.

It is possible that in the interpenetrating world of the future the most positive means of preserving national identities will be the continued expansion of educational opportunity because of the crucial role of knowledge in innovative capacity, a quality essential to foster in order to make distinctive national contributions to post-industrialism and so to maintain a national saliency, that is, to appear in the world as a society that does something particularly well. Canada's potential in this respect is partly dependent on the future of national science policy and its effects on research. Outside the field of science, the development of national culture – in the broad sense of a distinctive way of life as well as distinctive artistic expression – will also depend on the expansion of educational resources. Among the English-speaking provinces, Ontario, because of its wealth and its large French-speaking population, should lead in the development of francophone education at all levels as one dimension

---

[8] Bertram Gross, *The State of the Nation: Social Systems Accounting* (London: Tavistock, 1966), p. 80.

of the purpose of achieving a national identity through educational activities. These considerations take us well beyond the provinces as parts of Canada and raise questions that must be faced on the future role of the federal government in the financing and planning of post-secondary education.

There are many other aspects of the society of the future which are highly relevant to planning of post-secondary institutions. For example, students will have had quite different child-rearing and early educational experiences than in the past, and egalitarian ideology will no doubt be more strongly articulated with new demands for higher education as a social right. Because they are sources of innovation, and because they have great talents at their disposal, universities will be looked to more and more to provide guidance in a rapidly changing world, guidance which includes continuing critical appraisals of the present state of affairs. The institutions of higher learning must free themselves of vested interests in order to strengthen the entire society that sustains them rather than only privileged parts of that society.

Our focus throughout is upon trying to look ahead, to judge the *texture* of post-industrial society, the society in which our present students will live and for which the students of the future should be prepared. We reach no cut-and-dried conclusions. We are dealing impressionalistically with a long time-span and many imponderables. Most changes need to be phased in over a period of time; we have been concerned with the direction of change, not with its speed. In the Epilogue that concludes the brief, we have brought together our strongest convictions about the pattern of post-secondary education as we believe it should develop in the years ahead.

CHAPTER 2

THE
MARCH
OF
EVENTS

Post-secondary educational developments of the future must obviously build on the system existing at present. The history of the
Ontario system has been studied elsewhere.[1] Here we shall look
briefly at very recent changes so as to identify significant trends.
With the accelerated pace of change it is not necessarily relevant
to take a lengthy retrospective view, and we have chosen to compare the 1965-66 situation with the present. The changes since
1965-66 are numerous and important and as we shall see they reveal themselves in every sector of the system.

A word about the mechanism of change is appropriate. Unlike Quebec, Ontario has had no Parent Commission[2] to provide a master plan for its educational development. Changes in
Ontario have been evolutionary rather than revolutionary, and
have usually resulted from careful studies of one or other aspect

---

[1]Robin S. Harris, *Quiet Evolution* (Toronto: University of Toronto Press, 1967).
[2]*Report of the Royal Commission of Inquiry on Education in the Province of
Quebec* (Government of Quebec, 1963-1966).

of the system by competent groups. For instance, the training of
secondary and of elementary school teachers has been studied
and reported on by government-appointed committees; the
Grade 13 year in the secondary schools – a distinctive Ontario
feature – and the aims and objectives of education have been
similarly studied. The Commission on Post-Secondary Education, appointed in April 1969, is the latest in the series of government-appointed groups. Meanwhile, various aspects of the university and other post-secondary sectors have been examined
by academic groups, and publications such as the Deutsch,[3]
Spinks,[4] Macpherson,[5] and Morand.[6] Reports have been influ-
ential in planning and rationalization. This piecemeal approach to revision and reform has not the same impressive-
ness as Parent or Robbins, and it permits some parts of the
system to work at cross purposes with others from time to
time. Nevertheless the evidence indicates that it has not been
ineffective.

Universities

In striking contrast to the five-year period 1960-65, when degree-
granting charters were awarded to no less than five new institutions, no new universities have been established in Ontario in the
past five years. Indeed the number of universities has been reduced by one through the surrendering of its charter by the Osgoode Hall Law School on becoming the Faculty of Law of
York University in 1968. But while the number of universities in
the Ontario system has not increased, it is no exaggeration to say
that each has been radically transformed during the last five-
year period as a consequence of very substantial increases in enrolment of undergraduate, graduate and part-time students (see
Table A), and by the addition of new faculties, schools and
campuses.

---

[3] *Post-Secondary Education in Ontario 1962-1970* (Committee of Presidents of
Universities of Ontario, 1962).
[4] *Report of the Commission to Study the Development of Graduate Program in
Ontario Universities* (Toronto, November 1966).
[5] *Report of the Presidential Advisory Committee on Undergraduate Instruction in
the Faculty of Arts and Science, University of Toronto* (Toronto: University of
Toronto Press, 1967).
[6] *Undergraduate Student Aid and Accessibility in the Universities of Ontario* (Report of the Subcommittee on Student Aid to the Committee of Presidents of
Universities of Ontario, 1970).

Table A. Enrolments in Ontario Universities 1965-66 and 1969-70

| University | Full-Time | | | | Part-time | | | |
| | Undergraduate | | Graduate | | Undergraduate | | Graduate | |
	1965-66	1969-70	1965-66	1969-70	1965-66	1969-70	1965-66	1969-70
Brock	354	1,628	-	18	162	1,001	-	-
Carleton	2,737	5,995	287	701	2,272	1,352	234	488
Guelph	1,890	5,097	203	545	10	249	16	37
Lakehead	421	1,781	-	43	731	1,423	-	33
Laurentian	938	1,987	-	5	960	2,611	-	-
McMaster	3,252	5,666	520	1,008	3,240	2,524	422	510
Ottawa	3,424	5,430	561	1,245	1,888	5,184	-	2,095
Queen's	4,137	6,357	532	933	166	209	105	243
Toronto	14,701	20,196	3,029	4,703	4,553	5,013	757	2,350
Trent	278	1,270	4	5	4	437	2	1
Waterloo	3,917	9,166	511	1,308	445	347	41	225
Western	6,262	10,237	843	1,585	1,382	2,281	76	110
Windsor	2,175	4,314	176	506	81	2,294	46	193
York	1,447	7,149	36	585	1,911	4,422	-	654
Waterloo Lutheran	2,199	2,624	34	89	2,031	3,503	6	11
Total	48,132	88,897	6,736	13,279	19,836	32,850	1,705	6,950

Source: DBS Survey of Higher Education. Part I: Fall Enrolment in Universities and Colleges, 1965-66 and 1969-70, adapted to exclude theology, pre-matriculation, and certain other students. (Details of the adaptations appear in the CPUO brief to the Commission on Post-Secondary Education in Ontario, January, 1971, Table III-1).

One characteristic of the expansion during these five years has been the remarkably even distribution of the increase in terms of programs. The total full-time enrolment – graduate and undergraduate – has in effect doubled, as has been the case in arts and science and in graduate studies. Table B shows full time undergraduate enrolment figures. In theology there has been a decline; veterinary medicine is practically static; in agriculture and nursing, the increases are less than 15 per cent; in architecture (which now has substantial enrolments in landscape architecture and town planning), in education (essentially the training of secondary school teachers), in forestry, in library science, in music, in physical and health education, and in social work, the increases are striking.

Since 1965 a new medical school has been established at McMaster, and new facilities at Toronto have made it possible to increase considerably the size of the graduating class. Additional facilities have also been provided at Ottawa, Queen's and Western. The realization of the increased "production" provided for in the 1965-69 quinquennium will be fully achieved in 1975. Somewhat the same situation applies to dentistry since the new faculty at Western reaches capacity in 1972 and the planned graduate expansion at Toronto's Faculty of Dentistry is not complete.

The addition of a Faculty of Fine Arts at York University, which admitted its first students in September 1968, is worthy of special note. Hitherto, fine arts in Ontario universities has been essentially a liberal arts subject with general and honours courses concentrating on historical development and philosophic theory. The programs at York, which include dance, drama, film and music, as well as the plastic arts, while giving due emphasis to theory have also a heavy practical orientation, with perhaps three times as much "studio time" as in the older programs.

Teachers Colleges

Colleges for the training of elementary school teachers have declined in both their number and enrolment. These reductions are explained by the absorption, at the beginning of the 1969 session, of the École Normale by the University of Ottawa, and of the Lakehead Teachers College by Lakehead University, and

14

Program	1965-66	1969-70	New Programs (1969-70 Enrolments)
Arts and Science	31,641	57,163	
Agriculture	769	1,004	
Commerce. Bus. Admin.	2,168	3,261	Lakehead (77). York (47)
Architecture	239	516	Carleton (86). Waterloo (151)
Dentistry	485	585	Western Ontario (88)
Education	914	2,933	Queen's (219)
Engineering	5,631	8,747	
Fine Art	91	502	McMaster (55). Queen's (24). Western (92). Windsor (88). York (243)
Forestry	512	261	Lakehead (61)
Household Science	512	867	
Journalism	169	319	
Law	1,627	2,414	Windsor (141)
Library Science	180	483	Western (182)
Medicine	1,360	1,605	McMaster (20)
Music	284	661	McMaster (26). Queen's (26). Windsor (27)
Nursing	1,086	1,517	Lakehead (122). Laurentian (35)
Optometry	100	161	Waterloo (161)
Pharmacy	407	518	
Phys. Health Ed.	698	3,128	Guelph (172). Lakehead (74). Laurentian (131). York (53)
Physio. Occup. Therapy	270	441	Queen's (102). Western (40)
Secretarial Science	139	148	
Social Work	264	793	Laurentian (65). McMaster (143). Western (18). Waterloo Lutheran (78). Windsor (141)
Theology	1,215	913	
Vet. Medicine	285	280	
Others & Unclassified	567	545	Environmental Studies Waterloo (175). Community Planning Waterloo (200). Translation & Interpretation Laurentian (31) Religious Ed. & Religious Sci. McMaster (26). Toronto (65). Ottawa (16)
TOTAL	51,101	89,765	

Source: DBS Survey of Higher Education Part 1: Fall Enrolment in Universities and Colleges 1965-66 and 1969-70. See note to Table A.

by the raising in September 1969 of the admission requirements
for the one-year certificate course to the same level required for
admission to university. Both these developments reflect implementation of the 1966 Report of the Minister's Committee on
the Training of Elementary School Teachers, which recommended that by approximately 1975 all elementary school
teachers be required to hold a degree and that teacher training
for both elementary and secondary school teachers be provided
in Faculties of Education of universities. A further step was
taken in July 1970 when the Windsor Teachers College was
absorbed by the University of Windsor. From September 1971,
one year of university studies is the requirement for admission
to the one-year certificate course. Thus some portion of increased enrolments in universities is the result of a very lauda-
ble policy decision to improve the quality of teacher education.
The absorption of other teachers colleges in universities is
under active study, particularly at St. Catharines (Brock University) and Toronto Lakeshore (York University).

Colleges of Applied Arts and Technology

The most striking institutional development in the province
since 1965 is the conversion of the five institutes of technology
and the six vocational centres of that time into colleges of
applied arts and technology and the simultaneous establishment of new colleges. There are now twenty CAATs and in 1969-
70 their full-time enrolment of 37,813 represented more than
six times the number (6,161) enrolled in the institutes of technology and vocational centres in 1965. In actual fact, a claim
could be made that there are as many as one hundred CAATs in
Ontario since each of the twenty has a number of branches in
the region for which it has responsibility.

The extension of the number of locations in which CAAT
programs can be undertaken has been accompanied by an extension of the programs offered. The offerings of the institutes of
technology in 1965 were, in the main, engineering technology
(at all five), business administration (at four) and textile technology and industrial management at one – Hamilton. The vocational centres confined themselves to apprenticeship courses
in both certified and non-certified trades, to courses related to
the federal government manpower training programs, and to a
limited number of technician courses.

The apprenticeship and manpower training programs (which remain a special federal concern) are now offered in the CAATs . Programs in engineering technology and business administration are offered at all the CAATs but in addition all have developed courses in an impressive variety of other fields. The example of one of the smaller CAATs, Georgian at Barrie, is typical. Its 1969-70 enrolment was as follows:

Art and Interior Design	60
Business Administration	51
Civil Technology	8
Electrical Technician	8
Electronic Technician	34
Electronic Technology	10
Engineering Technology	38
General Arts and Science	4
General Business	46
General Secretarial	48
Legal Secretarial	5
Mechanical Drafting Technician	10
Mechanical Technology	8
Medical Secretarial	17
Resort Operation	37
Resource Technology	10
Retail Merchandising	8
Survey Technician	12
	414

At Humber, one of the larger CAATs, no less than forty-four programs were offered in 1969 including architectural design, chef training, computer programming, early childhood education, hotel and restaurant administration, nursing, public relations, and recreation leadership.

In 1969, half of the CAATs were offering two or three year courses in general arts and science, and these numbers can be expected to increase. It must also be noted that arts and science subjects are important in almost all CAAT programs, particularly those categorized as applied arts.

Programs in which French is the language of instruction are offered only at Algonquin (Ottawa), and only in certain fields so far. Algonquin's stated objective is to become fully bilingual by 1975. The Cornwall campus of St. Lawrence is considering French courses.

Students enrolled in the apprenticeship program attend the CAATs on a full-time basis for a two month period in each of three years but they have not been included in the full-time enrolments given above. In addition to these there were 34,978 part-time students in the CAATs in 1969-70.

Ryerson Polytechnical Institute

Considerable expansion of its physical plant has meant that both full-time and part-time enrolment at Ryerson has nearly doubled in the five years since September 1965. In contrast to the other institutes of technology of the 1960-65 period Ryerson offered a much broader range of programs – home economics, architecture, radio and television arts, secretarial science, journalism, furniture and interior design, photographic arts, medical laboratory technician training, printing, and courses for sanitary inspectors, as well as various branches of engineering technology and business administration. It continues to offer these programs but it is also now a school of nursing and has expanded its offerings substantially in the paramedical fields, aerospace technology, urban planning, library arts, social work and landscape technology; and it is developing its English and Philosophy Departments to a larger extent than many of the CAATs have done.

Colleges of Agricultural Technology

In 1965 there were three Schools of Agriculture – at Kemptville in Eastern Ontario, at Ridgetown in Western Ontario, and at Guelph, the latter the non-degree division of the old Ontario Agricultural College, which became the University of Guelph in 1964. Since then additional colleges of agricultural technology have been established at New Liskeard and Centralia.

The course at Guelph is offered on a contract basis between the Department of Agriculture and the University of Guelph. The Department has also made arrangements with Fanshawe College of Applied Arts and Technology at London to provide the agricultural technology course at centres which Fanshawe has established at Woodstock and Simcoe. In addition there is the Niagara Parks Commission School of Horticulture at Niagara Falls.

Schools of Nursing

Fourteen of the seventy-two schools of nursing are no longer admitting students to the first year of the three year course. Two "schools" are now located in educational institutions – one at Ryerson Polytechnical Institute and one at Humber College of Applied Arts and Technology (there are also nursing assistants programs at two other CAATs, Niagara and Seneca) and it is likely that this trend will accelerate. The most significant development, however, is a reorganization of the three-year course which now concentrates the academic work in the first two years, with the third and final year becoming in effect an internship, and it is very likely that the course itself will soon be reduced to two years. The 1969 enrolment figure included ninety-seven males, a significant increase from 1965.

Other Professional Schools

There has been a modest increase in the enrolment of the Ontario College of Art – from 928 in 1965 to 1,027 in 1969. The Forest Ranger School in Dorset, which had been operated by the Department of Lands and Forests since 1946, became an in-service training centre for the Department in 1968, with the introduction of two-year courses in forest technology at three of the colleges of applied arts and technology. The Canadian Memorial Chiropractic College, a private as distinct from a public institution, has new and much improved quarters in Toronto and continues to enrol just over 200 students. There has been no change in the number of private theological colleges and seminaries, nor in their total enrolments. The noticeable decline in the number of private trade schools registered in the province and of their total enrolment is undoubtedly due to the provision of comparable courses in the colleges of applied arts and technology.

The Significant Trends since 1965

This review of developments since 1965 enables us to note certain significant trends:

1. a movement away from the single purpose professional or vocational school, evidenced by the absorption of Osgoode Hall Law School by York University and of the Ontario College of Optometry by Waterloo, by the trans-

19

fer of forest technology courses from the Ranger School to the CAATs and by the assumption of responsibility for the course for registered nurses by institutions other than hospitals;

2. an enormous expansion of the number of locations where post-secondary education is available, evidenced not only by the doubling of the number of CAATs, but also by additional university campuses (Toronto, Laurentian, York) and new colleges of agricultural technology at New Liskeard and Centralia;

3. a substantial increase in the number of university students enrolled in and graduating from professional courses, as well as a continuation of the increase in arts and science;

4. a substantial increase in the range of technological courses offered;

5. a substantial increase in the enrolment of part-time students, at the universities, at Ryerson, and in the CAATs .

Two other significant developments of this five-year period have not been mentioned: the establishment in 1966 of the Ontario Institute for Studies in Education, and the opening in September 1970 of an educational television channel in Toronto. The effect of the addition of OISE is already apparent in the greatly increased number of students registered for graduate courses in education at the University of Toronto, with which the Institute is affiliated. Less obvious at this stage is the effect the Institute will have on the Ontario educational system, including post-secondary education, as the result of the research undertaken by its staff. All that can be said at this point is that Institute staff is engaged in both research and development in the area of post-secondary education, and that the potential value of the Institute's contribution is great.

Since the first educational television channel has been operating for only a handful of months, and since to date programming has been confined to the elementary and secondary school level and to adult programs of a general nature, its contribution to the post-secondary system must also be described as potential. It is, however, a new element in the system and one of obvious importance.

Present Institutional Structures and Interrelations

One of the objectives in presenting this review of developments in the post-secondary educational system of Ontario is to reveal its complexity. It is, clearly, a very complex system involving several hundred institutions, thousands of administrators, tens of thousands of teachers, and over 300,000 full and part-time students. Elsewhere we shall have something to say about the size and complexity of its financing. What requires attention here is a brief outline covering organization and interrelations.

Responsibility for the system rests ultimately with the Legislature of the Province but is borne primarily by two government departments, Education and University Affairs. However, a number of other departments, notably Agriculture, Health and Labour, are also involved, either directly or in conjunction with Education or University Affairs. In addition the government has established three bodies to advise it on matters related to the development of specific parts of the post-secondary educational system.

The *Committee on University Affairs*, established in 1961, is a group of up to twelve persons who advise the government on all matters concerning the establishment, development, operation, expansion and financing of universities in Ontario. The *Ontario Council of Regents for Colleges of Applied Arts and Technology* is a body of fifteen persons authorized by the 1965 Act which created these colleges, with responsibilities comparable to those of the Committee on University Affairs with respect to the universities. The *Ontario Council of Health* whose seventeen members include the Deputy Minister of Health (who acts as chairman), the chairman of the Ontario Hospital Services Commission and representatives of the medical, dental, pharmacy and nursing professions, and also laymen, was established in 1966 as the senior advisory body on health matters to the Minister of Health and the Government. Its terms of reference include "health resources development and maintenance, including the health services required for education and training, services and research." One other body must also be mentioned in this general description of governmental arrangements for the organization of post-secondary education in Ontario, the *Senior Coordinating Committee for the Health Sciences*, which consists of various officials concerned with educa-

21

tion and health. Their task is to review the plans and needs of each university and to develop a coordinated plan for the development of the health sciences of Ontario.

Relations between the Committee on University Affairs (CUA) and the Department of University Affairs (DUA) are close. The structure of the Department remains essentially the same as it was when it was created in 1964 – deputy minister, assistant deputy minister, and senior officials responsible for branches concerned with architectural services, finance, research, and student aid. The most significant change since 1965 in the Committee on University Affairs was the appointment in 1967 of a full-time chairman from the academic world. The policy introduced in 1964 of appointing active members of the teaching and administrative staffs of Ontario universities to the Committee has been continued.

The CUA advises the Government on matters related to the universities, and the DUA executes the policies which the Government adopts. Each university is at liberty to attempt to influence the Government's policies with respect to its role in the system through discussion with either of these bodies, but in addition there are three bodies which concern themselves with the needs of the Ontario universities as a group. The oldest of these is the Committee of Presidents of Universities of Ontario (CPUO) which was formed in 1962. Besides the fourteen Presidents there are fourteen Senate-appointed representatives of the universities, an Executive Director, a Research Director, and a small staff. In 1965 CPUO had a half-dozen sub-committees appointed to deal with particular problems, with membership drawn from the academic and administrative staffs of the various universities. In 1970 the number of committees was twenty. Examples are the Council on Admissions, which has developed a common form of application for admission and a system of coordinated admission practices, and the Ontario Council on Graduate Studies, which has worked out a successful method for the appraisal of graduate courses and a means of obtaining objective assessments of entire disciplines or groups of disciplines.

The Ontario Confederation of University Faculty Associations (OCUFA) is the second of the intra-university organizations. Founded in 1963, it now consists of the faculty associations of the fifteen Ontario universities, the combined membership of which embraces over 90 per cent of the teaching staff. OCUFA presents briefs to the Government on specific issues from time to time, and since 1969 has presented an annual submission to the Committee on University Affairs.

The third body is the Ontario Union of Students, founded in 1964. In theory a parallel body to OCUFA, its capacity to represent the student point of view has been reduced in recent years by the withdrawal of the Student Councils of two of the largest universities in the Province.

The Department of Education has jurisdiction over the teachers colleges, the CAATs and Ryerson Polytechnical Institute. The latter, however, is what is called a ministerial agency, and this in effect means that though it is a responsibility of the Minister, it is only nominally a responsibility of the Department. Executive responsibility in this case lies with Ryerson's Board of Governors, and in this sense its position is parallel to that of the universities.

There is also a Board of Governors for each of the CAATs, but their situation is not parallel to that of the universities for two reasons. First, the Council of Regents has a more direct responsibility for the individual CAATs than has the CUA for the individual universities. Second, the Applied Arts and Technology Branch of the Department of Education plays a much more direct role in the determination of policy at the CAATs than does the Department of University Affairs with respect to the universities. The reason for this is historical. Several of the Ontario universities had been in existence for a century when the Department of University Affairs was created in 1964, and even the most recent foundations were staffed by persons who had long experience in university matters. But when the legislation creating the CAATs was passed in 1965, there were relatively few persons in Ontario with extensive experience of how institutes of technology should be run and even fewer with experience in the kind of institution which the CAAT was intended to be. None the less within three years twenty CAATs were in operation and it is not surprising that in this situation many of the decisions that had to be made, about curricula for example, were actually made by the officials of the Applied Arts and Technology Branch. With several years of operation behind them the CAATs have acquired a good deal of experience and the role of the Applied Arts and Technology Branch is increasingly that of providing advice rather than direction. There is also now a Committee of Presidents of Colleges of Applied Arts and Technology of Ontario, paralleling CPUO.

The teachers colleges are the direct responsibility of the Teacher Training Branch of the Department of Education. Here there are no boards of governors for the individual college or any body comparable to the CUA or the Council of Regents, and the courses of study vary little between colleges.

Clearly a good deal of progress has been made since 1965 in the structural organization of post-secondary education in Ontario. But there is still further progress to be made. Organizational problems include the isolation of some teachers' colleges and the near total communication gap between all but a few of the CAATs and the universities.

What has been said so far is that the Ontario post-secondary system has changed substantially during the past few years through expansion of enrolment, numbers of institutions, types of institutions and structural organization. It could be argued, however, that, the introduction of the CAATs excepted, such changes are simply more of the same. But the fact is that the most significant changes in the system since 1965 are in the area of the attitudes of the persons involved in the system. This is particularly noticeable in the case of students, but it is also apparent in the case of teachers and professors, of administrators and support staff, of government officials, and of the public at large. We turn to these matters in the following chapter.

CHAPTER 3

THE
ALTERATION
OF
ROLES

The attitude of the public at large to the universities of Ontario
is entirely hostile, and the bigger the university the greater the
hostility – or so some journalists would have us believe. There
has certainly been much questioning of functions and procedures. Expressions of editorial outrage were for a time directed
mainly against university students and university presidents.
Now the professors are under fire for downgrading their teaching duties, the tradition of academic tenure is called in question,
expansion of university libraries is attacked, and research, especially fundamental research, is stigmatized as a wasteful luxury
that impinges on the main job of teaching. Thus every one of
the traditional functions of the university – the dissemination,
preservation and advancement of knowledge – is challenged in
one way or another.

Questioning of this sort is healthy, and is not by any means
confined to those outside the universities. How meaningful today is the old notion that the functions of the university are to
preserve, disseminate and extend knowledge? In the post-industrial, knowledge-based society it is increasingly urgent for

these functions to be performed somewhere, but it does not necessarily follow that all must be performed in any one kind of
institution.

Why are so many young people coming to university? No
doubt at one time they came if not in passion at least in the
good-natured habit of their class. But as the system developed to
take in more of them, increasing emphasis was placed on career-
ist values and higher earnings. The notion of higher education as
the royal road to success was fostered particularly in the period
immediately after the Second World War, and it led to and encouraged the ideal of equality of educational opportunity. More
recently, however, there has been a shift from the "investment in
oneself" orientation to that of consumption. Education is doing
things as well as preparing oneself to do things, it is having
experiences as well as anticipating experiences. The system dis-
penses experiences besides disseminating knowledge. Experience
and learning go together.

Systems of higher education will have to provide for these new
orientations as increasingly their students become more selective, have rising expectations, and are more ready to reject authority. Students, however, will never be a homogeneous group;
there will always be some who will be dedicated to learning for
its own sake, and who will accept authoritative relations as helpful to that end. Students, in other words, will have different
needs. Clearly the post-secondary system as a whole must be
multi-functional and highly differentiated.

When students look at the university's role in society they see
it as reinforcing the existing order. Recently universities have
been much criticized for being the servants of the existing power system and the vested interests of the dominant social class.
Many of these criticisms have force. The conflict between the
traditional view of the university and the radical view has been
clearly articulated in *Toward Community in University Government*, the report of the 1969 Commission on University Government of the University of Toronto. The traditional view is
of the university as primarily an academic institution serving
the historic functions:

> In this view, students are considered to be engaged in
> two main areas of university activity – one academic,
> the other social. In his academic role, the student is

26

an apprentice who has come to the university to study under a master. It is very much an old-style guild relationship. As such, the gap in age, intellectual attainment and professional expertise makes the student largely passive in everything that has to do with academic organization and decision-making. In his social role, however, the student plays an active part. . .

The university, in this view, does not adopt a political posture towards the "outside" society. . . .The university's relations with society at large are strictly at arms' length . . . the university is defined by its academic rather than its social role; its organization and structure are dictated by the needs of academic disciplines, not by social or political considerations. Its ethos is individualistic, not collective.[1]

The radical view is of the university as a social institution, one that cannot and, in fact, does not work in an intellectual or social vacuum. The radical is extremely critical of both the university and the society. He focuses on the economic and social functions of the university, what is taught and how it is taught, and what research is done there. He points out that most students come from middle and upper class homes, and concludes that the university is a class institution, training the young of an economic elite to continue to perform that role, and providing a source of mobility for those from middle class homes to join the elite.

From the perspective of this radical critique, the problem is to establish a genuinely critical university, a university that would, as a community, combat the tremendous homogenizing and managerial tendencies that develop in the technocratic university. Alienation and distrust amongst students and faculty are clearly not going to disappear overnight; the university is only part of society, a par-

[1]*Toward Community in University Government* (Toronto: University of Toronto Press, 1970), pp. 27-8.

tial environment. But the objective of the radical persists – the creation of a humane, cooperative community in a democratic society.

Thus, radicals see a different role for the university in society at large, as well as quite different relationships within the university community itself. The two goals are integral: the university must no longer be merely the pale reflection and servant of the market society, but an independent and critical force; patterns of authority and status that smother genuine criticism and the development of real intellectual enquiry must be broken down inside the university as well as outside.... The task for the democratic university is to give students and staff the ability to control the decisions that affect them, i.e. to give them the means to make the university critical.[2]

Although the radicals have not made it clear how social ends are better served by giving students and faculty power to control their work situation, we can anticipate a continuation of a radical and critical component within not only the university, but all higher educational institutions. In fact some leading universities now compete for the more able of the radical young professors, and in many learned societies there are radical counter organizations. Fashions of radicalism and criticism will no doubt change, but since post-industrialism offers greater opportunities for planning and a greater choice of alternatives, much more critical analysis of social conditions and public policies will be necessary. Thus it is important to add this critical function to those which the university has traditionally had. Moreover within a differentiated educational system this may be a function which is assigned primarily to universities to perform. It is not a new function – universities have been offering critical analyses of social conditions for centuries. What is new is the urgency of the need.

We have seen in recent years rising impatience with the slow response of our political, bureaucratic and other elites in dealing

---

[2] *Ibid.*, pp. 31-2.

IT IS UNLIKELY THAT THE PROFESSOR OF THE FUTURE WILL WORK IN THE SAME
CAREER PATTERN

with the problems of the time. This impatience has expressed itself in sharper tones of dissent than formerly, and has led in
some cases to illegal and violent acts. Predictably, these have
bred a reactionary impatience with dissent itself. In this climate,
society must be particularly alert to preserve and safeguard the
freedom of outspoken criticism.

The Professors of the Future

Not only are changes taking place in the university as a social institution, but also the roles and relationships of those who make
up the university community are changing. It is unlikely that the
professor of the future will work in the same career pattern as
the professor of the past. There will not be the same kind of relationships with his employer (university or college), with his students and colleagues, or with society. The model of the ivory-
towering scholar-professor working to a great extent by himself
and subject to very little control other than that imposed by his
own standards is firmly implanted. It was no doubt an appropriate model during the elitist phase when only a small proportion
of young people went to university. For some professors it will
probably continue to be a working life style, but it is scarcely
suitable as a general model for a future system approaching
mass higher education. It is worth reviewing some of the changes
which might occur, considering current trends, but before doing
so it will be well to deal briefly with a related matter – the supply
of academic manpower.

In many respects the staffing of the Ontario universities has
been remarkable, considering the recent expansion. Most of our
universities have been competitive in the academic market-place.
Although there has been much criticism of the heavy reliance on
the recruitment of non-Canadians, it would have been impossible to have reached our present stage of development using only
our own resources of manpower. A great many additional staff
members will be required for the post-secondary system, especially if part-time, adult and continuing education in addition to
full-time numbers develop as we expect. By the same token, the
pool from which staff members of the future can be drawn is
very large. With the transition from elitism to democratization
in higher education, the base is substantially widened.

Thus our own graduate schools should become increasingly

29

the source of recruitment, although care must be taken to avoid a rampant nationalism which would destroy some of the benefits of drawing from the international intellectual community. One advantage, incidentally, of the decline of the bull market for Ph.D. holders is the prospect of improving the level of faculty talent; recruiting committees can become more selective.

The position of professor is an attractive one and seems likely to remain so. Professors, like teachers generally, are either reasonably well paid or else well paid, and the work itself is attractive to those who are drawn to teaching. Ideally the professor is teaching a subject he likes to students who are mature enough to contribute themselves to the elucidation of the subject, and the opportunity is provided him for further investigation of those aspects of the subject that interest him most. Moreover, the conditions of work are on the whole excellent. While a great deal of nonsense has been spoken on the subject of the four-month summer holiday and the nine-hour working week, it is a fact that the university teacher is remarkably free to schedule his work to suit his own convenience. His is an onerous task, but how and when it shall be accomplished is within his powers to decide. The conditions of work are also attractive in another sense – the fact that the university professor is or can be functionally involved in the determination of institutional policy. He is not an employee who simply does what his employers order him to do.

In theory, then, there should be no problem in ensuring adequate numbers of university teachers in the future. In practice, however, there are a number of problems arising from the complex nature of the university professor's work, the relatively long period of time required to qualify oneself for the position, and the changes (which we would like to explore) that may be expected as both scale and differentiation develop within the Ontario post-secondary system.

One of the changes we are likely to see is a diminution in the relative numbers of professor-scholars. There will be a variety of ways of being a teacher within this emerging post-secondary system. The traditional role of the professor-scholar cannot be discarded because, as we have already pointed out, the universities' concern for excellence will continue. We would anticipate that the most exciting and advanced work will still be done by

30

creative minds working alone or being left alone to bring together the creative teams (including advanced students) that are necessary to make breakthroughs in many fields. What is *not* likely is that the entire system will be manned by workers conforming to this model. For one thing, at that level of creativity there are not that number of people of such high quality. Yet all the additional staff that have been taken on by universities in the recent expansion have been recruited with this model in mind. The result in some cases has been low teaching loads and the right to a lot of free time to engage in research; and it is unfortunately true that much of this research is not very important and only sees publication in journals of low quality – journals which proliferate to meet demands for media for publication. In this "publication pollution" there is, we feel sure, some kind of professorial "Peter Principle" at work.

Some professors find research a burden and would be happy to be relieved of it in favour of teaching. In many respects universities themselves are to blame for the situation that has arisen because they have made publication a *sine qua non* of promotion, at the same time placing a lesser value on teaching. We would hope, therefore, to see those who prefer to teach – not simply a few students in a cozy seminar, but larger classes as well – rewarded adequately in promotion and pay for doing so. At the other extreme is the pure researcher working at very advanced levels of inquiry, who may have few teaching duties. This last type of worker might be located in research institutes outside universities. Depending on how research is financed – a subject that we consider later on – the pure researcher may in the future be less of a burden on university budgets.

It would seem necessary to offer opportunities in graduate school programs for candidates to discover whether their interests lie mainly in research, in a combination of teaching and research, or in teaching alone. In the last-named case a teaching oriented degree such as the Master of Philosophy or the oft-proposed Doctor of Arts might be appropriate. Every effort should be made to direct young graduate students to the work for which they feel best suited. It may not be possible to avoid distinctions in status between the star researcher and the college teacher, but it should be possible to provide within the post-secondary system a teaching career which is rewarding both in status and remuneration.

31

Another change in academic life-styles may result from a professional development similar to what has taken place in medicine, a switch from the solo practitioner to a team approach to the "delivery" of services, and a greater interest in systematizing and evaluating the process of interaction – in the academic's case, the teaching-learning process.

Another change concerns the participation of professors in university government, and more recently still the sharing of governmental responsibilities with students – although it remains to be seen whether the student interest of the past few years in joining governing bodies will prove to be permanent or ephemeral. Along with government we would include administration of faculties, departments, etc. With the increasing size and resulting operational complexity of universities, the number of administrative tasks has so increased that almost all staff members (under the present arrangements) must for certain hours of the week, or for certain years in their careers, turn their attention to administrative matters. As with the teaching function, little attention is paid in graduate school programs to this administrative role.

The question could well be asked whether or not the university teacher has an obligation to do administrative work, and if so to what extent? Related to this problem are the extensive networks of committees in which almost all university personnel eventually become entangled. How many man-hours of high-priced help are spent in committee discussions? It should be possible to rationalize much of this palaver without the loss of faculty control and responsibility. In many cases, committees of academics are attempting to perform administrative functions instead of making policy. Perhaps we need, as the Economic Council of Canada has suggested, new programs to train university administrators who could do much of the preparatory work of committees, and who would also carry out committee decisions much as in a governmental civil service. We would also expect that a number of professors would opt, as they do at present, for administrative work. Since they are aware of the special institutional character of universities they will probably continue to be the best source of recruits either for special training programs or for gradual transfer to administrative functions.

Tenure and Collective Bargaining

We would anticipate that the present skirmishing around the professorial bastion of tenure will develop into a major assault. Contrary to widely held views tenure has not had a particularly long history in Ontario. What we have seen over the past few years, with a bull market situation for professors, is a more easily obtained and an earlier granting of tenure under rules worked out between administrations and increasingly strong faculty associations.

From the point of view of the professoriate the argument for tenure is that it is a mechanism to protect from political or other pressures or from arbitrary dismissal the scholar whose views, developed in the search for truth, might well come into conflict with those of the wider society or those in power (which often means the same thing). This may well become an outmoded argument for tenure. Even though we live in a politically volatile atmosphere now and will probably continue to do so, and even though Canada seems to be starting to experience a more authoritarian climate, it is doubtful that tenure as it now exists is necessary to safeguard professors, or that it is the only effective mechanism against arbitrary dismissal.

There is no reason why properly constituted dismissal proceedings with all the necessary due process cannot be devised for all forms of academic misconduct. Nor is it impossible to draw up a code of professional ethics with reference to which academic misconduct can be judged. All of the traditional academic freedoms can be embodied in such a code. Tenure is usually obtained on the grounds of scholarly merit and is similar to a licensing procedure – and one, incidentally, which has to be obtained only once, early in the career. Professors will never argue that tenure protects them from dismissal on the grounds of scholarly demerit or loss of scholarly standing; it is *infra dig.* to mention such things, once the license has been obtained.

From the point of view of many outside the university, and, it must be admitted, from the sheer economic considerations in a labour intensive industry, tenure is something of an absurdity and an unusual privilege. It has the appearance of a protective cover for feather-bedding with surplus professors clinging to their jobs or becoming inefficient or indolent. Up to the present time it is not likely that feather-bedding has resulted from tenure because it is unlikely that a smaller number of professors would have been required, given the expansion of the past decade. Moreover, with the improved market situation the university can be concerned with quality rather than quantity; hence the "productivity" of the professoriate as a whole should be improved. Academic productivity is one of the most elusive of measures, but we would speculate that if teaching were to become a more valued part of the system than in the past, as we have suggested, some efficiencies would result.

Where the cold economic argument seems to be greatest is with the conditions which are likely to prevail in the future; among these, perhaps the most important is professorial obsolescence. This is a human problem as well as an economic and an organizational one. Let us consider these problems.

Unless a university or a department is well up in standing with the top fifteen or so institutions of the world, it is likely that many of its professors will fall behind the developing fronts of their disciplines. We assume that Ontario will not be able to support more than one or two major institutions of the first rank that would match, for instance, universities ranked high in the recent study of the American Council on Education. At the same time it is likely that our recruitment policies will continue to place a high value on the doctoral students from those leading institutions, particularly returning Canadians. These younger, more recently trained faculty with, generally speaking, their creative life before them can easily come into conflict with the fifty-year-olds entering a phase of obsolescence because their own graduate training took place twenty years before and they have lost contact with changes in their discipline. Without some form of security they might well be pushed out by the more aggressive of their younger colleagues. This condition is most likely to arise in the rapidly developing disciplines in the fields of science and social science.

A similar problem arises with redundant professors, those for whose subject there is a falling demand. With freer student choices, subject popularity could well run through peak and trough cycles of ten years or so, and the result could be a surplus of professors hired to satisfy a high level of demand that has since fallen off. There may also be problems with unpopular professors who may be subject to student disfavour

34

if students acquire strong voices on matters of professorial personnel policies. Thus obsolescence, redundancy and popularity
are relatively recent aspects of the tenure problem and have
nothing to do with tenure's original purpose.

Clearly obsolescence and redundancy lead to "economic
inefficiencies" in the educational system. There are a variety of
ways of dealing with these diseconomies. It is a fact that a
once-in-a-lifetime certification of professional practitioners is
becoming inappropriate to a world of rapid change and explo-
sive knowledge. Professors also may need to retool themselves
in the course of their working lives. The present pattern of
sabbatical leaves lends itself to this development – more liberal
provision of leave with pay could do much to increase academic productivity as well as increasing personal satisfaction. In
making this suggestion we ask no more for professors than we
would ask for all professionals. Indeed, there is much to be said
for a "citizens' sabbatical," a period of study leave earned
regularly by everyone who contributes positively to the good of
society, to help all useful people to keep up with the pace of
change.

The solution to the problem of professorial redundancy, on
the other hand, may lie in revising the graduate school programs in such a way that the possibility of changing disciplines
is improved from the outset. Less intense specialization, and
built-in provisions for the wider, more philosophic approach,
are clearly the key.

Another possibility for the academic world is that a pattern
of retirement earlier than the present norm will become general
in this and other occupations. The indicators are already developing in industry and government: for example, the recently
concluded agreement in the automobile industry provides that
a person is retired on full pension after thirty years' service,
and the new policy of the federal civil service of Canada is for
retirement at age fifty-five after thirty years' service. It may be
that we shall see a different age span for participation in the
labour force. Rapid changes of the future may well require
retiring the older, less productive people and replacing them by
the younger and more productive. Although earlier retirement
may appear to be an additional burden for the economy, the
costs might well be met by the more productive and more
flexible work force that would result.

If early retirement for professors becomes normal, those who retire will doubtless find creative uses for their time, as their high level of training would enable them to keep active in ways which may not be available to others. The idea of early retirement runs counter to cherished images of an honoured academic venerability, but we think that this possibility, along with the others we have sketched, should be carefully studied by educational planners.

The important thing that should be done is to define more accurately the role of the university professor, to spell out what is in fact expected of him. Clarification of these matters would assist the graduate student who wants to continue in academic work to decide in which career direction he wished to move, and it would enable the graduate schools to adapt their programs to the reality of the eventual situation of such students. It would also contribute immeasurably to the more effective operation of departments, and indeed of universities.

Tenure may well be replaced by some form of collective agreement arrived at through established practices in other occupations where collective bargaining has been used. If this should horrify professors, it should be remembered that many professional groups do bargain collectively, and with the emergence of medical care plans even physicians are having to enter into such situations. Collective bargaining may, however, create more problems than it solves with respect to improving the productivity within the academic system. Any agreement would have to cover a wide range of academic activity. As one observer has noted:

> Previously unwritten practices now become formalized in highly specific contractual arrangements. The equipment of the office, the number of students per class, the schedule of classes to be taught during the day, the academic calendar, these and other matters now become contractual considerations.[3]

It is easy to imagine that the policing of such agreements and the process of settling grievances and disputes could become

---

[3]R. E. Blackburn, "Changes in Faculty Life Styles," *Research Report No. 1,* American Association for Higher Education.

both time-consuming and complex. But perhaps the big contra-
diction in collective bargaining in universities is the situation in
which the professors, through representative mechanisms within the university, control much of their own working conditions. Under present circumstances they could in effect be
bargaining with themselves. Besides, it is a well established
practice within the university that many professors should par-
ticipate in many "management" functions. Often the academic
administrator is appointed on a term basis and rotates back to
being a professor. In fact it is often considered important to
grant some credit for administrative activity in considering promotion and salary.

However, even though the scope of a professor's work and
the "colleague" type of relationship throughout the university
are somewhat unusual, it should not be impossible to take
account of these things in a collective agreement, either on an
institutional or a provincial level. In some jurisdictions such
agreements already exist. We would suggest a thorough study
of them and perhaps a joint attempt with OCUFA to devise a
model collective agreement. Such an undertaking would not
require any group to adopt it. It would be an exploratory
study.

As well as covering salary, working conditions, retirement
and other forms of severance, etc., collective agreements should
embody protection for the traditional academic freedoms.
Thought should be given to whether these various matters
would be better negotiated at the systems level or at the individual university level. System-wide bargaining would do something to prevent universities from bidding against each other,
although in the final analysis academic salaries are determined
by wider market conditions. The main advantage of system-
wide bargaining would be the removal from individual universities of the possible conflict between colleague-administrator
and professor-employee.

If and when collective bargaining becomes the pattern, there
should, we believe, be an important exception: top-level professors should bargain for themselves. The reason for this is that it
might be impossible to bid in the international market within
the restrictions of collective bargaining arrangements, and we
do not want to see Ontario universities so inflexible that they
cannot stretch a point to get their share of the very best. Those

professors at the highest level of human endeavour and creativity can make arrangements about their own contracts as executives do in business.

Finally, there may be a need to rethink the whole concept of the university teacher, not simply in relation to teaching, research and administration in the university, but as well in the context of society as it is developing. Is the currently held concept based on a free enterprise system and a capitalist economy, and is it valid for either a welfare state or a socialist society? If it is so based and if Ontario is headed in the 1970's or 1980's in either of the last two directions, we must ask ourselves what the appropriate role of the professor of the future will be – and that of the student of the future as well.

The Students of the Future

The freshmen of September 1970 differed substantially from their opposite numbers in 1965. All the Ontario high school graduates who were admitted to universities in 1965 had sat the Grade 13 Departmental Examinations which were then the sole criterion of admission. By 1970, Departmental Examinations had been abolished and admission was based on recommendations from the individual secondary schools and on objective tests. The effect of this change was twofold. First, as had been argued by the Minister's Grade 13 Study Committee of 1964, effective control of Grade 13 was assumed by the classroom teacher, who no longer was obligated to prepare students for an examination that others would set, with the result that freedom rather than restriction began to characterize the classroom situation. Secondly, the freeing of the Grade 13 curricula encouraged experimentation not only in the Grade 13 year but also in the lower grades. This development was further encouraged by the publication in 1968 of *Living and Learning*, the Report of the Committee on the Aims and Objectives of Education in the Schools of Ontario (Hall-Dennis), which the Minister of Education had appointed in 1965.[4] Both instruction and curriculum in most schools in the province differ noticeably in

---

[4] *Living and Learning*, The Report of the Committee on Aims and Objectives of Education in the Schools of Ontario (Toronto: Newton Publishing Co., 1968).

1970 from 1965, and the differences will be more marked as the 1970's advance.

These changes have necessitated a re-thinking of the courses of study in the post-secondary institutions, since the base which they could assume (such and such a standard in chemistry or French, for example) is no longer automatic. But even before this had become necessary the winds of change had whistled through the university corridors and re-examination of the curricula became the order of the day. The consequences are typified by what occurred at the University of Toronto between 1966 and 1969 – the introduction of a New Program in Arts and Science, replacing the honours and general course system which had been in very solid existence for close to a century, and entirely new curricula in Medicine, Architecture, and Law. The key word here is "typified"; the changes at Toronto are, or are likely to be, rivalled or surpassed by changes elsewhere. For both student and professor the consequences have been comparable to those experienced by students and teachers in Grade 13.

In 1966 the Duff-Berdahl report, *University Government in Canada*, devoted two and a half of its one hundred pages to the role of students in the governance of universities.[5] A year, even six months later, the student role would unquestionably have received ten times as much attention. This is a reminder of how recent is the emergence of the student power movement as a potent factor in the educational affairs of the province. It is also a reminder of how great the differences are between the situation five years ago and today. It is now normal for students to be functionally involved in the making of policy at the departmental and faculty level of most, if not all, universities in Ontario. In many cases students are also involved at Senate level, and in some instances at Board level. Students at the CAATs are similarly involved. It is both appropriate and inevitable that students should be represented as full members of the Commission on Post-Secondary Education in Ontario. In general, university administrators and government officials have recognized the justice of the increased involvement of students

---

[5]Sir James Duff and Robert O. Berdahl, *University Government in Canada* (Toronto: University of Toronto Press, 1966).

in decisions affecting the nature and quality of their educational experience. But many people still question it. One reads that
aggressiveness on the part of those *in statu pupillari* is wrong,
that student interests and indignations are transient and short-
lived, and that it is concessions on the part of weak-kneed
elders that are really responsible for student unrest: if we would
only reassert old-fashioned discipline, it is said, there will be no
trouble. We need not look far outside our borders to see that
attitude of avuncular sternness escalated to hatred and fear,
and repressive measures carried to tragic lengths. How shall we
come to grips with this problem? Can we help those outside the
university to understand the concerns of modern students? Can
we understand them ourselves?

The students of the future are here already, but we have been
slow to recognize them. We have been calling them a minority,
but they are a vanguard. They are the first representatives of
what Margaret Mead calls the prefigurative culture – children
who face a future that is so deeply unknown that it cannot be
handled as a generation change within a stable, elder-con-
trolled, parentally modelled culture. We have seen already that
the only certainty before us is accelerated change. Dr. Mead,
whose studies of the acculturation of young people have been
lifelong and world-wide, has said:

> Today, suddenly, because all the peoples of the
> world are part of one electronically based, intercom-
> municating network, young people everywhere share
> a kind of experience that none of the elders ever
> have had or will have. Conversely, the older genera-
> tion will never see repeated in the lives of young
> people their own unprecedented experience of se-
> quentially emerging change. This break between
> generations is wholly new: it is planetary and uni-
> versal.[6]

The students of the future are far more mature and knowl-
edgeable than those of the past. Today, according to Dr. Hugo
McPherson, 19-year-old college entrants have seen more than

---

[6]Margaret Mead, *Culture and Commitment, A Study of the Generation Gap*
(Garden City, N.Y.: Natural History Press, Doubleday & Co., 1970), p. 64.

five hundred feature films, viewed some 15,000 hours of television, and have read perhaps fifty books on their own initiative. We face, Dr. McPherson says, a new kind of person in our universities and high schools – a person who has more information about the world than his parents had in middle age.[7]

The students of the future are also biologically farther advanced for their age than were those of the past: there is ample documentation for the earlier onset of adolescence, earlier menstruation, growth spurt, etc., and the progressive speeding-up of the whole process of growth. The magnitude of this trend is considerable, dwarfing, for instance, the effect upon growth of differences between socio-economic classes.[8] Students are also becoming more in balance with the sex ratio in the population as women are beginning to catch up – the rate of increase of female students is higher than the male rate. This will in itself change the patterns of enrolment, including graduate and professional fields, and the coming into force of the Ontario Women's Equal Opportunity Act (on 1 Dec. 1970) will almost certainly reinforce such enrolment changes. A result of the larger numbers of women graduates will be heavy competition in the narrow range of professions where women have been traditionally accepted, unless women enlarge the range of occupations for which they prepare. The United States Labor Department has already called attention to this possibility. The Royal Commission on the Status of Women in Canada has in its Report forcibly brought to the attention of both educators and employers the changing role of women in the occupational world.

The students of the future will come from a wider socioeconomic spectrum than those of the past. More of the groups who are now under-represented in post-secondary institutions will be encouraged and enabled to attend, and the existing remnants of a preponderance of WASP attitudes and values will diminish and probably disappear.

The students of the future will increasingly come from schools where (as has just been mentioned) freedom rather than

---

[7]Hugo McPherson, "The Future of Literary Studies and the Media," *Transactions of the Royal Society of Canada*, Series IV, Vol. VII, 1969, p. 248.
[8]J. M. Tanner, *Growth at Adolescence* (Oxford: Blackwell Scientific Publications, 1962), p. 143.

restriction characterizes the classroom situation: schools, that is, where the herding together of individuals into homogeneous "grades" and the isolation of different elements of experience into water-tight "subjects" are becoming outmoded, and where the evaluation of competence solely by formal, uniform, time-limited written "examinations" will soon be as outlandish as trial by ordeal. These students will not be conditioned to regard a teacher in the role of a godlike person pouring out facts which the masses are expected to take down word for word. They will not be seeking nuggets of knowledge, but rather the ability to get knowledge when needed, to interpret it and collate it and use it. They will learn by dialogue – questioning, challenging, arguing. They will learn by recognizing patterns and taking in many things simultaneously, rather than through a compartmentalized structure of subjects and disciplines and a sequential series of courses. We are moving away from the situation so severely criticized by McLuhan:

> The young today live mythically and in depth. But they encounter instruction in situations organized by means of classified information – subjects are unrelated, they are visually conceived in terms of a blueprint. Many of our institutions suppress all the natural direct experience of youth, who respond with untaught delight to the poetry and the beauty of the new technological environment, the environment of popular culture. It could be their door to all past achievement if studied as an active (and not necessarily benign) force.[9]

The students of the future will be accustomed to cybernetics and large-scale space-age problem-solving. They will be interested in human and humane applications of cybernetics – the solution of environmental problems, the allocation of planetary resources throughout the global village. If they can be assured, or even hopeful, about technology being under human democratic control, most of them will not look at technology in

---

[9]Marshall McLuhan, *The Medium is the Massage* (New York, London, Toronto: Bantam Books, 1967), p. 100.

ignorance, distaste or fear; they will recognize it as a vitally necessary tool for coping with the great planning problems we have already mentioned, that are bequeathed to them from the industrial period. They will agree with the young scientist who said not long ago that the cure for misapplied technology is not to be found in a panic-stricken flight from technology, but in well-applied technology.[10] For *Canadian* students of the future with a new concern for Canada as a nation there will be a particular set of national problems that they will have to find the tools to solve; their concern will be to seek an alternative to the miniature replica of American society that Canada is in such danger of becoming.

The students of the future will probably be more politically adroit than those of the past, more adept at exploiting the university's, and society's, divisions. They may be more cynical, more ruthless, more violent, more retaliatory. On the other hand they may be more idealistic, more dedicated to service, gentler. (Which kind of people they are will doubtless depend on what their experience has led them to expect from the adult world.) It is true that some of them will follow fashions of protest and use slogans with small regard to their meaning. Some now call for *relevance* with no reflection on the level of individual capacity to find things relevant; some demand *accountability, parity,* etc., with little appreciation of the tenuous balance of the democratic process on its foundation of mutually agreed assumptions; and these will be succeeded by new catchwords. Student discontent will remain a constant factor for a long time; rationalization of it will vary.

The students of the future will seek more direct experience, experience through the senses, than those of the past. It is noted in *Living and Learning* that "our youth are evincing a desire to experience things more through the senses, and this desire manifests itself in several new patterns of behavior – not the least of which are the use of psychedelic drugs, earlier and more gregarious sexual experience, more noise, more color, more movement, creating a brash, vibrant, kaleidoscopic, 'go-

---

[10]J. C. Polanyi, Convocation Address at the University of Waterloo, May 29, 1970.

go' world."[11] Some will be unable to handle the freedom they
demand and will become slaves of self-chosen masters, self-
destructive, wrecking mind and body. Some will get lost in
their search for a reality that they can believe in – in their
probing and rediscovery of an "inner" world. "As a whole
generation of men," writes Dr. R. D. Laing, "we are so es-
tranged from the inner world that there are many arguing that
it does not exist; and that even if it does exist, it does not
matter. Even if it has some significance, it is not the hard stuff
of science, and if it is not, then let's make it hard. Let it be
measured and counted."[12]

The students will be impatient with our habitual compart-
mentalization of man's capacities, with our splitting of what
Erich Fromm calls cerebral-intellectual function from affective-
emotional experience. Already many of them have an understanding of the *reunited* personality that Laing and Fromm are
striving to describe. "Logical thought," Fromm writes, "is not
rational if it is merely logical and not guided by the concern for
life, and by the inquiry into the total process of living in all its
concreteness and with all its contradictions."[13] It follows that
the students may not be willing to accept without serious questioning the attitude that we have been brought up to regard as
academic respectability, but which they may see as academic
arrogance. The adulation of the mind – the worship and trust
of the intellect alone – may seem to them idolatrous and perv-
erse when set against their concept of the whole man. Already
their half-amused preoccupations with astrology, witchcraft
and drug-induced experience argue a certain sense of wonder, a
sense of the numinous, a call for the human intellect to be
humble in the presence of a world that seems to exhibit beauty
and mystery beyond the intellect's powers of apprehension and
understanding. (This is not the same as a flight from the intellect: to opt out of the process and the pain of rational thinking
is a diminishment of the whole man, not a fulfilment.)

---

[11]*Living and Learning*, p. 28.
[12]R. D. Laing, *The Politics of Experience* (London: Penguin Books, 1967),
p. 46.
[13]E. Fromm, *The Revolution of Hope* (New York: Bantam Books, 1968), p. 42.

The students of the future have grown up without the reliance that many of their elders had been able to place during their early formative years on religion, on family, on patriotism, on the authority of experienced persons, on an ethical system embracing absolute values, even on an unformulated assumption that during threescore years and ten spring will succeed winter, birds will return and rain will refresh. In an article called "The Revolt of the Diminished Man," Archibald MacLeish has written:

> The distress, the very real and generous suffering and distress of an entire generation of young men and young women is related certainly to the miseries of the Sixties, but it is not founded in them and it will not disappear when they vanish – when, if ever, the war ends and the hot summers find cool shade and the assassinations cease. The 'relevance' these students speak of . . . is relevance to their own lives, to the living of their lives, to themselves as men and women living.[14]

Their consciousness has changed. Their perceptions are different. Their way of handling experience is different. This has happened quickly, but not overnight – some observers, notably Marshall McLuhan, have been trying for more than a decade to make people understand the extent and completeness of the change and to abandon "the witless repetitive response to the unperceived."[15] There is no use trying to change the students back again, as is proved by the failure of the most brutal measures of repression. They are full citizens of their world, whereas older people are immigrants in that world, as Margaret Mead says – immigrants in time.

The students of the future will demand of post-secondary education a return to a vision of man as a whole. One virtue the generation of the young does possess (MacLeish points out) to a degree not equalled by any generation in this century: it

---

[14]Archibald MacLeish, "The Revolt of the Diminished Man," *Saturday Review*, June 7, 1969, p. 18.
[15]McLuhan, *op. cit.*, p. 10.

believes in man. They will demand that the college and the university should stand "not as a bastion of the Establishment ... but rather as a stronghold of authentic humanism, a champion of that belief in man which is the best hope to-day for the university and the world."[16]

---

[16]D. R. G. Owen, *Provost's Annual Report*, Trinity College, Toronto, 1969, p. 13.

CHAPTER 4

THE
POWER
OF
NUMBERS

Having tried in the last chapter to describe attitudes, we now turn to the more prosaic but scarcely more certain area of numbers.[1] In this chapter we attempt to place some quantitative parameters on the challenge of expansion which will face Ontario's post-secondary system in the next decade. We do not project beyond 1980 leaving the patterns of that period quite properly to be determined from decisions made in the 1970's.

We approach the task of anticipating enrolment growth with considerable trepidation. Anyone familiar with the inherent methodological difficulties and the history of enrolment projections in Canada will realize how risky a business this is. Uncertain projections are inevitable in an essentially open system where the government has established the policy of responding to social demand. Student preferences shift over time in ways

---

[1] We owe a debt of gratitude to Mr. G. Grant Clarke for assistance in the writing of this chapter and chapter 11 and to Mr. Terry DaSilva for statistical tables and projections.

47

which are difficult to anticipate since they are part of the whole fabric of the value system of our society. Besides this, various changes in public policy – for example, the upgrading of requirements for elementary teacher certification – can markedly alter the picture. Since future policy changes cannot be anticipated, we have based the projections in this chapter on the premise of a continuation of present government policies.

The Development of the Ontario University System in the 1960's

The decade of the sixties was one well described by the Economic Council of Canada as "vigorous educational mobilization."[2] Both government and the universities responded resourcefully to the considerable challenge of vastly increased educational opportunity for the young people of Ontario. In the rapid pace of development which has characterized all regions of Canada, Ontario has maintained a position of pre-eminence. A few statistics will remind us how dramatically the university part of that system expanded in the past ten years.

In 1960-61, there were just under 29,000 full-time students in the provincially-assisted universities. In 1970-71, there were over 111,000, an almost fourfold increase over the decade. This growth (an average of over 14 per cent a year) reflects the compounding effect of increased university-age population and a participation rate (of the 18-24 year age group) which more than doubled over the decade. Growth rates in undergraduate and graduate enrolment in Ontario have been almost identical; in 1960-61 graduate enrolment represented 11.5 per cent of the total full-time enrolment; in 1970-71 it was 12 per cent of the total. Accurate comparable statistics on part-time enrolments are not available but we have estimated part-time winter session enrolment in 1960-61 to have been between 9,000 and 10,000 students, and about 50,000 in 1970-71. Thus, part-time enrolments grew even faster than full-time during the decade.

Data on enrolment by program of study are available only in gross categories but certain general trends can be detected. Undergraduate enrolment in 1960-61 was about equally divided

---

[2]Economic Council of Canada, *Sixth Annual Review: Perspective 1975* (Ottawa: Queen's Printer, 1969), p. 124.

between arts/science and professional programs. In the sixties, enrolment in arts/science programs rose much more rapidly than in the applied disciplines. In 1965-66, arts/science enrolment reached 60 per cent of the total, and over the next several years it stabilized at around 64 per cent. Growth in arts and science was close-to-linear, and growth in professional programs accelerated during the latter part of the decade.

The pattern was somewhat different in the graduate area. Arts and science programs accounted for a relatively constant percentage of the total over the decade, about 60 per cent of total enrolments. Within that proportion, there was a slight shift from science to arts.

Anticipated Patterns of Enrolment Growth in the 1970's

Table C shows estimates of total full-time enrolment in Ontario from 1968-69 to 1980-81. Two of these projections, the lowest and highest, were taken from a publication of the Ontario Institute for Studies in Education (hereinafter termed "OISE").[3] A third projection included here is that undertaken for the Economic Council of Canada (hereinafter termed "EC").[4]

These are based on historical enrolment statistics from the Dominion Bureau of Statistics (DBS), which include students in other than the provincially-assisted universities. Adjustments must therefore be made before these figures can be compared with actual enrolments available from the Ontario Department of University Affairs (DUA). Thus, wherever a comparison between DUA and DBS statistics becomes necessary, the DUA figures have been adjusted upwards by an appropriate factor. In addition, EC projections, unlike those of OISE, include enrolment in teachers' colleges with the university enrolments from 1968-69 onwards. Teacher education will ultimately be completely integrated with the universities so we have added the

---

[3] *Ontario University and College Enrolment Projections to 1981-82* (1968 projection) by C. Watson and S. Quazi, Department of Educational Planning, Enrolment Projection Series No. 4, The Ontario Institute for Studies in Education.
[4] *Enrolment in Educational Institutions by Province, 1951-52 to 1980-81* by Z. E. Zsigmond and C. J. Wenaas; Staff Study No. 25 prepared for the Economic Council of Canada, January 1970.

estimated enrolment of teachers' colleges to both of the OISE projections rather than subtracting them from that of the EC.

Which of the three projections is most deserving of our confidence? If we compare the actual enrolment in 1968-69, 1969-70, 1970-71 (column 7 of Table C) with those projections which were undertaken by OISE and the EC back in 1967 and 1968, we see that all three estimates were surpassed. The main reason for this is that the participation rate[5] of the university-age population (18-24 age group) increased from 9 per cent in 1965-66 to 13.6 per cent in 1970-71. EC expects the participation rate to be 18.9 per cent in 1975-76 and 22.8 per cent in 1980-81 – slightly higher than is projected by OISE in their highest projection, and thus, based on our recent experience, the EC enrolment projection is more realistic.

It can hardly be over-emphasized how sensitive these projections are to the participation rate assumed. It is our opinion that the EC estimate is more likely to hold in the future than the OISE estimate, and further that it may turn out to be an under-estimate of social demand.

There are extraneous factors, not capable of being included in a statistical projection, which could have enormous effects on actual enrolments. Some factors would retard the increase. For example, alarm at job prospects for graduate students during 1970 depressed enrolments at the graduate level. Cutbacks in graduate student aid programs for 1970-71 and 1971-72 have had their effects on graduate enrolment.[6] Limitations in capital funding could cause universities squeezed for space to react by raising admission standards, thereby closing the "open door."

Attitudes toward the value of a university education could markedly affect enrolment up as well as down. Policies could be established by government (such as the increased educational requirements for elementary teaching) which would increase

---

[5] That is, the percentage of the total age group who are registered in colleges and universities.
[6] The Ontario Graduate fellowship program was funded at $6 million in 1969-70; for 1970-71 $5 million were made available, and for 1971-72 not more than $3.5 million is expected to be made available.

Table C. Total full-time projected enrolment (000's)

	(1)	(2)	(3)	(4)	(5)	(6)	(7)
Year	OISE No. 1B	OISE No. 2A	Teachers' Colleges *	OISE No. 1B Including Teachers	OISE No. 2A Including Teachers	Economic Council	Adjusted Actual Plus Teachers
68-69	88.9	91.0	10.9	99.8	101.9	101.9	103.5
69-70	100.5	104.2	12.0	112.5	116.2	114.0	117.2
70-71	112.1	117.1	11.5	123.6	128.6	124.8	129.3**
71-72	123.9	129.5	8.5	132.4	138.0	137.4	—
72-73	135.2	140.4	9.7	144.9	150.1	153.0	—
73-74	146.5	152.1	9.7	156.2	161.8	167.5	—
74-75	156.8	165.6	9.3	166.1	174.9	186.0	—
75-76	166.3	178.8	10.1	176.4	188.9	202.7	—
76-77	175.4	192.4	10.9	186.3	203.3	217.9	—
77-78	183.2	205.8	11.7	194.9	217.5	234.7	—
78-79	190.8	218.0	12.4	203.2	230.4	248.0	—
79-80	198.2	229.8	13.3	211.5	243.1	266.0	—
80-81	205.6	239.8	14.0	219.6	253.8	280.0	—

* The Teacher Education Branch, Ontario Dept. of Education, has projected a levelling-off of the demand for new teachers from teachers' colleges to just over 8000 from 1971-72 on. However, we anticipate some increase in this level as a result of demand for improvement in teacher/pupil ratios, particularly at the elementary level, although pressure on costs might slow this otherwise desirable process.

** Anticipated actual.

the numbers requiring university education. Similarly, the professions could exert pressure on their members to upgrade or renew their qualifications periodically at institutions of higher learning. Also, the change in sex ratio noted in the last chapter points to an over-all increase unless the additional women are coming *instead of* their brothers, which seems unlikely. For certain people, too, irrespective of background, social status, income group, etc., a taste of education whets the appetite for more. If the teaching facilities are available close by, inexpensive, and open at convenient hours, and if the program can be extended over a period of years of part-time study, the dream of democratization, of near-open access to a university education, may become a reality. (Witness the open admissions policy adopted at the City University of New York in 1970-71). All of these are imponderables which make the forecasting process a very risky business.

Supply and Demand Comparisons

It is desirable to relate capacity of the university system to demand in terms of the *types* of places required, so we have utilized broad discipline groupings for these comparisons. (It would be even more desirable of course to look at actual disciplines rather than broad groupings, but data are not available at this level of detail. Also, the margin of error with finer groupings would be much greater.)

The discipline groupings employed are those used by the Dominion Bureau of Statistics and are as follows:

1. Arts[7]
2. Pure Science[7]
3. Applied Social Sciences – Commerce and Business Administration, Household Science, Law, Physical and Health Education, Secretarial Science, Social Work
4. Applied Physical Sciences – Architecture, Engineering

---

[7]Enrolments in "Arts" are as designated by the universities reporting to DBS. It appears that in the case of undergraduate enrolments, but not graduate, this category in fact represents arts and science for most universities. The pure science category would be accounted for by those universities which have separate faculties of science.

5. Applied Biological Sciences – Agriculture, Dentistry, Forestry, Nursing, Optometry, Pharmacy, Physical and Occupational Therapy, Veterinary Science
6. Applied Humanities – Fine Art, Journalism, Library Science, Music, Theology
7. Medicine
8. Education

The actual percentages of enrolment distributions among these groups were calculated from DBS data for the last seven years. These percentages are shown in Table D, for full-time undergraduate, part-time undergraduate and full-time equivalent of part-time enrolment.

Significant inferences about prospects for growth may be detected in (a) the relative rates of growth of graduate and undergraduate enrolment within broad disciplinary categories; (b) the changing rate of growth of part-time students, (c) the influence of policy statements such as the decision to require a university education for all school teachers; and (d) the dampening effects on enrolment resulting from the feedback of information on supply and demand for university graduates in the marketplace. All of these have implications for the future and can be taken into account to add some refinement to our crystal ball-gazing into the future.

It is readily apparent, for example, that while the full-time undergraduate enrolment percentage in Arts and Pure Science is reasonably stable, there have been definite decreases in Applied Physical Sciences, Applied Biological Sciences and Medicine and increases in Education, Applied Social Sciences and Applied Humanities. Any limited-enrolment subjects will, of course, decrease as a percentage of the whole if other components are growing. The far right column of Table D contains best-guess percentage distributions for 1975-76.

The Economic Council estimated enrolments for 1975-76 in Table C were disaggregated to show full-time undergraduate, full-time graduate and full-time equivalent of part-time students. Best-guess percentage distributions for 1975-76 were then applied to these enrolment estimates to get the "demand" figures by discipline group in Table E.

For capacity projections we shall assume that the capacity of the university system in any given year is determined by the forecasts of enrolments made by the universities five years ear-

53

lier and thus that the capacity in 1975-76 will be determined by
the 1970-71 university forecasts. (We have not projected capacity beyond 1975-76 since university forecasts beyond that point
are not available.) It is reasonable to relate capacity to university forecasts because capital monies are allocated by the Province using a weighted student formula which calculates space
entitlement on the basis of these rolling five-year university
forecasts. Thus, if there are no significant changes in the capital
formula and if no universities are in a space debit condition
(i.e., owe space to government) at the end of the period, the
universities' five-year projections of enrolment should closely
approximate the physical capacity (supply of student places) of
the system five years later.

The anticipated supply of student places by discipline group-
ing was obtained by applying the same best-guess percentage
distributions to the adjusted university enrolment forecasts.
These figures are shown in the supply column of Table E. Our
total demand estimate for full-time undergraduate places in
1975-76 is 176,400, while only 146,300 places are expected to be
available in the existing university system. In the Arts category
(which includes Science for most universities – see footnote 7),
82,900 places are likely to be required, and our estimated supply reaches only 68,700.

Thus, we estimate that *by 1975-76, if participation rates follow recent trends (i.e. the "open-door" policy is continued), there
will be an unfilled demand for 30,100 full-time undergraduate
student places, almost half of these being in Arts and Science.*
Even in Pure Science, which has been projected to be on the
decrease, there will be an unfilled demand for 4,800 student
places. About 17 per cent of the total full-time undergraduate
student demand will remain unsatisfied in 1975-76. For full-
time graduate and part-time students, despite the greater elas-
ticity in these areas at some universities, we estimate the excess
of demand over supply in 1975-76 to be 5,800 and 2,400 full-
time equivalent students respectively. These are areas, however,
in which normal demands can easily be distorted by restrictive
public policies.

The dimensions of the anticipated shortfall in undergraduate
student places may be appreciated by noting that the numbers
represent the equivalent of a university larger than the University of Toronto (about 19,000 full-time undergraduate students)

Table D. Percentage distributions by discipline group

Full-Time Undergraduate

Discipline Groups	63-64	66-67	69-70	Estimated 75-76
Arts	41.4	46.4	46.6	47.0
Pure Science	13.1	16.3	16.7	16.0
Subtotal	54.5	62.7	63.3	63.0
Applied Physical Science	13.7	12.7	10.9	10.0
Applied Social Science	12.4	10.6	11.3	11.0
Applied Bio Sciences	9.8	6.8	5.7	7.0
Applied Humanities	2.6	1.8	3.0	5.0
Education	2.1	1.9	3.5	3.0 *
Medicine	4.9	3.5	2.2	1.0
TOTAL	100.0	100.0	100.0	100.0

Full-Time Graduate

Discipline Groups	63-64	66-67	69-70	Estimated 75-76
Arts	35.6	37.6	37.2	38.0
Pure Science	24.7	25.6	23.3	21.0
Subtotal	60.3	63.2	60.5	59.0
Applied Physical Science	12.7	15.0	13.8	12.0
Applied Social Science	10.3	9.4	12.4	14.0
Applied Bio Sciences	4.7	3.5	3.0	5.0
Applied Humanities	2.4	0.7	2.2	3.0
Education	1.4	2.5	4.1	5.0
Medicine	8.4	5.8	4.1	2.0
TOTAL	100.0	100.0	100.0	100.0

Total Part-Time Head Count

Discipline Groups	63-64	66-67	69-70	Estimated 75-76
Arts	80.3	83.0	77.8	78.0
Pure Science	1.7	2.1	5.3	5.0
Subtotal	82.0	85.1	83.1	83.0
Applied Physical Science	1.2	1.4	1.6	1.0
Applied Social Science	11.2	7.6	6.6	6.0
Applied Bio Sciences	1.0	1.9	1.2	1.2
Applied Humanities	0.8	0.7	0.8	0.7
Education	3.6	3.3	6.6	8.0
Medicine	0.1	0.1	0.1	0.1
TOTAL	100.0	100.0	100.0	100.0

* Excludes teachers' colleges in 1975-76

being created within the next five years. It also might be noted that although we have presented a supply/demand comparison only for 1975-76, a deficit appears in 1971-72 and grows steadily thereafter. We should stress that these are *university* places for which requirements have been estimated. There is no indication that the rapid expansion of other post-secondary opportunities in the past several years has had any significant effect in reducing the demand for university places. Nor do we expect this to be the case in the foreseeable future, except insofar as a shift in responsibilities and/or an increase in transferability may take place.

It may be that certain universities, as they become aware of this potential demand, will be prepared to revise their forecasts upwards. In certain cases where this is possible, however, it would involve creation of new campus sites. Even talking about the situation in which we shall find ourselves in 1975-76 is fraught with uncertainty, and, as we have pointed out, it may be that demand for university places will grow more slowly or more quickly than we have suggested in the preceding pages. Nonetheless, the capacity of the existing institutions in the university system to expand further will become severely limited at least by the middle of the 1970's. In considering possible alternatives for providing additional places, the fundamental question is whether any further expansion should be contemplated along the pattern of the past decade, or whether some rather different alternatives ought to be considered.

Projected Enrolments in Non-University Post-Secondary Institutions

In attempting to project enrolments in the non-university part of the post-secondary system, we must climb out on a limb which is even shakier than in the case of the universities. The creation of the system of Colleges of Applied Arts and Technology just a few years ago gives us a very limited base from which to undertake projections. However, it may be useful to offer some views on the possible order of magnitude of other post-secondary enrolments to complement those we have undertaken for the university sector.

In attempting to project post-secondary non-university enrolments, we began by obtaining as many figures as we could

Table E. Estimated demand for and supply of student places in 1975-76 (000's)

		Demand	Supply	Shortage
Arts	Full-time UG	82.9	68.7	14.2
	Full-time G	10.0	7.8	2.2
	FTE of Part-time	21.7	19.8	1.9
	Total	114.6	96.3	18.3
Pure Science	Full-time UG	28.2	23.4	4.8
	Full-time G	5.5	4.3	1.2
	FTE of Part-time	1.4	1.3	0.1
	Total	35.1	29.0	6.1
Applied Physical Science	Full-time UG	17.6	14.6	3.0
	Full-time G	3.2	2.5	0.7
	FTE of Part-time	0.3	0.3	0.0
	Total	21.1	17.4	3.7
Applied Social Science	Full-time UG	19.4	16.1	3.3
	Full-time G	3.7	2.9	0.8
	FTE of Part-time	1.7	1.5	0.2
	Total	24.8	20.5	4.3
Applied Biological Sciences	Full-time UG	12.3	10.3	2.0
	Full-time G	1.3	1.0	0.3
	FTE of Part-time	0.3	0.3	0.0
	Total	13.9	11.6	2.3
Applied Humanities	Full-time UG	8.8	7.3	1.5
	Full-time G	0.8	0.6	0.2
	FTE of Part-time	0.2	0.2	0.0
	Total	9.8	8.1	1.7
Education	Full-time UG	5.3	4.4	0.9
	Full-time G	1.3	1.0	0.3
	FTE of Part-time	2.2	2.0	0.2
	Total	8.8	7.4	1.4
Medicine	Full-time UG	1.8	1.5	0.3
	Full-time G	0.5	0.4	0.1
	FTE of Part-time	0.0	0.0	0.0
	Total	2.3	1.9	0.4
TOTAL	Full-time UG	176.4	146.3	30.1
	Full-time G	26.3	20.5	5.8
	FTE of Part-time	27.8	25.4	2.4
	Total	230.5	192.2	38.3

from officials connected with the various institutions, and then supplemented these with interpolations and extrapolations as necessary.[8] The CAAT projections (SUM) appear to us to be on the high side and for planning purposes we favour the EC estimates of total non-university post-secondary enrolments. The EC projections show 86,000 students in non-university post-secondary institutions in 1975-76, of whom about 58,000 would be in the CAATs. The figure would be substantially greater if the expectations of the CAATs themselves were fulfilled.

Post-secondary Enrolment and Participation Rates in 1980

So far in this chapter we have examined various projections of post-secondary enrolments in universities and elsewhere. Our examination has led us to give most confidence to the projections undertaken by Zsigmond and Wenaas for the Economic Council of Canada. These projections show university full-time enrolments of 280,000 students and non-university enrolments of 115,000 for a total of nearly 400,000 post-secondary students by 1980-81. Post-secondary enrolment in both the university and non-university sectors would be about 2½ times its present size, which would mean growth rates of just over 8 per cent a year. This should be compared with the growth of the past decade which saw university enrolment nearly quadrupled (14 per cent a year), and non-university enrolment slightly more than tripled (12 per cent a year).

The common way of looking at enrolments in higher education is to establish "participation rates" of given age groups. These participation rates are artificial to the extent that actual enrolments fall beyond the age group chosen, but they still have some use as analytical measures. We believe that participation rates as conventionally defined for higher education (the 18-21 or 18-24 age group) will become increasingly less meaningful over the next decade. *We are clearly moving in the direction of lifelong education in the post-industrial society,* and institutions of higher education will less and less be dominated by a

---

[8] The details of these estimates are contained in the CPUO brief to the Commission on Post-Secondary Education in Ontario, January, 1971.

Figure 4-1 Full-time Post-secondary Non-university Enrolments

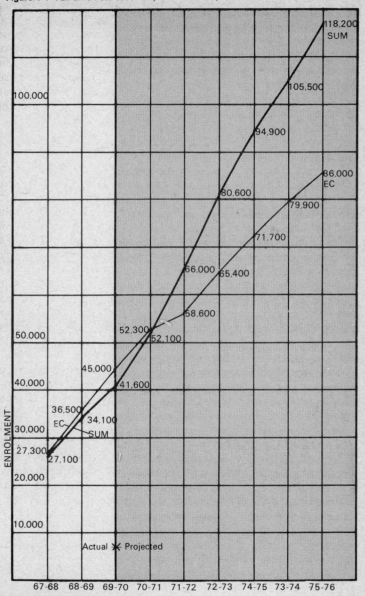

narrow age group as the decade progresses. In fact, we anticipate that the measure of adequacy of an educational system will change from the proportion of a given age group attending to the proportion of the *labour force* attending.

In the 1970's we expect that most of the increase in enrolment of older persons in higher education will take place on a part-time basis. We do not expect that part-time enrolments (which we think will grow more rapidly than full-time) will have any significant effect in depressing full-time enrolments. This expectation could be altered, of course, by policy decisions or radical changes in attitudes which would make part-time education really equal to full-time education in the amount of financial support and the quality of academic resources made available.

With these qualifications in mind, it may be useful to look at the likely participation rates assumed in the levels of enrolment projected for 1980. In 1960-61 post-secondary enrolments in Ontario were 9.0 per cent of the 18-24 age group, which by 1970-71 had increased by 120 per cent to 19.6 per cent. The figure projected for 1980 is 32.2 per cent of the 18-24 age group – an expected increase of only 65 per cent. Thus, we estimate that the participation in post-secondary education will continue to rise but at a rate slower than in the past decade. On the other hand increased accessibility and such factors as the greatly increased participation of women in post-secondary education might make our projections unduly conservative. And to some extent the participation will depend on the degree of our own creative imagination applied to future needs.

CHAPTER 5

THE MODEL
OF
ACCESSIBLE
HIERARCHY

We have seen from the preceding chapter that there is nothing in past trends or present indicators to lead us to expect a stabilizing of post-secondary enrolments, though the rate of increase may be slower from now to 1980 than it has been in the decade just ended.

The last chapter described the task of post-secondary institutions in terms of *numbers* of students, young and old. About the essential *content* of that task there is a large measure of agreement. Somewhere in the post-secondary system knowledge must be "preserved" – in libraries, increasingly on film and videotape, and in data banks; somewhere it must be advanced, theoretically and in practical applications; it must be applied to the direct service of society and brought critically to bear on society's institutions and ethics; and it must be transmitted to the young and to citizens of all ages who need it. There would also be general agreement that the knowledge to be transmitted includes the theory-based studies usually referred to as arts and science, or as liberal and/or general education, at various levels, and also the practice-based studies usually called technical, technological or paraprofessional, and professional – again, at various levels. The argument is always with respect to emphasis: whether teaching/learning is primary and research secondary, or vice versa; where the lines should be drawn between liberal, general and professional education; whether critical analyses of social institutions should be made only by the individual members of the academic community as individuals, or whether the community itself should offer such criticisms as a corporate body.

About the *locus* of the task, it should be noted that although universities have traditionally carried on these activities, no one of them is an activity which only universities perform. Libraries preserve knowledge, elementary and secondary schools transmit knowledge, research institutes and myriad individuals not connected with universities advance knowledge. Liberal or general education is carried on at the secondary as well as the post-secondary level, and professional training takes place in many non-degree-granting institutions – the Ontario College of Art and the Canadian Memorial Chiropractic College are convenient Ontario examples. Pure research may be carried on in industrial laboratories, and applied research is, of course, pursued in that setting. Governments serve society, and so, in a sense, do churches and corner grocery stores. Newspaper editorials, magazine articles, the CBC criticize society. If there were no universities in Ontario in 1980 or 1990, these services now rendered by the universities of the province would still be rendered in the province; whether they would be rendered on the scale or at the level of quality required is another matter.

What is unique about a university as an institution is that it performs all these services and has been doing so for close to a thousand years. Nor is this an accident. Experience over this period has shown that the preserving, transmitting and advancing of knowledge and the activity of critical social analysis can be most effective in certain areas when carried on in unison. But one should not therefore assume that this will be the case forever. In fact, we have already seen how other institutions – the CAATs for example – have taken on some of these tasks to good effect.

A further point is that no one of these activities can be regarded as an undifferentiated whole. To take research as an example: there is a distinction between pure (or theoretical)

62

research and applied (or practical) research. With respect to professional education, one must first recognize (in the area, for example, of engineering) a distinction between the technological and the professional level, and then between the basic professional degree level and the level of subsequent professional specialization. In all professional fields, furthermore, one must recognize a newly urgent need for still another area, that of continuing education – the additional education the active professional practitioner will need to acquire in order to keep abreast of new developments and new concepts in his field.

In the area of general or liberal education, there have been many attempts to define these terms and to distinguish between them. It is often said, for example, that the idea of liberal education, which is the older term, was developed at a time when a relatively small and sociologically homogeneous group of students attended universities, and that general education is simply the adaptation of liberal education for a much larger and sociologically less homogeneous group. However that may be, it does seem to be true that there are two sorts of education that should be provided for in the Ontario system, whether one labels them general/liberal, pass/honours, or generalist/specialist, or simply different degrees of concentration within a wide spectrum.

There is a kind of education that is concerned with the development of certain skills (such as the capacity to express oneself effectively in speech and on paper, to read efficiently, to solve problems, to evaluate information and reason from it) and the attainment of a thorough orientation to the world of knowledge and of affairs. The characteristic of this kind of education is breadth rather than depth, which is not to imply superficiality or the absence of discipline and serious purpose. It is the education appropriate to the thoughtful citizen, whatever his vocation. For convenience we shall call this *generalist* education.

There is also a kind of education that involves an earlier commitment to the mastery of a particular discipline or group of disciplines. Its characteristic is depth rather than breadth. It is very important because it meets the needs of those with an early, certain, and exclusive commitment to the discipline of their choice. Another purpose of this kind of education is to enable the rare, totally dedicated individual, including the genius or near-genius, to develop himself. Such people are a precious asset of any society, and although it is difficult or impossible to measure the likely incidence of "geniusness" or to give odds on its occurrence in a given setting or to do a cost-benefit analysis of educational programs that retain, perhaps uneconomically, a capacity for stretch and thrust beyond the average, we believe that in the Ontario post-secondary system individuals of truly exceptional potential should be catered to. We shall refer to this second kind of education as *specialist* education.

For a time it may be difficult to avoid elitist connotations in connection with specialist education because of its similarity to the traditional honours courses. These were a notable characteristic of Ontario, and had as one of their objectives the production of a certain cast of mind which as Milton phrased it three centuries ago would enable the possessor to perform "justly, skillfully and magnanimously all the offices both public and private of peace and war." For Milton as for Newman the liberally educated man was fitted to play a leadership role in society. All societies require leaders and there is nothing undemocratic about providing education that is aimed at producing the characteristics that leaders will need, so long as admission to the program is not based on social or economic discrimination and so long as the completion of such a program does not become a *sine qua non* for a leadership role. By linking up generalist education with an M.A. program that permits later concentration, we can ensure that the values of "in depth" study are made widely available.

In addition, somewhere in the system, or at least somewhere in Canada, there should be places where there are scholars who have specialized in the various languages and cultures of the world, and scientists who are expert enough to be working at the expanding edge of the known. In the "one world" of post-industrialism these kinds of expertise will be needed, and we do not think that Canada should remain in ignorance or ride on the coattails of other countries. Indeed there is for Canada a possibility of leadership, of true national saliency, in the educational challenge of the future. Often it is said that we cannot take a leading position in the fields of endeavour that are prohibitively expensive: we are unlikely, for instance, ever to compete with the Americans and Russians in outer space. But we can create an educational system of strength and renown, if we make that a national priority. We can excel in the exploration of the realm of the mind and heart, and in the development of capacity to handle complex knowledge which will be increasingly important as we move towards 2000.

We must remember, also, that the post-industrial society will be much more leisure oriented, and we shall therefore need to increase greatly the opportunities for education in art, drama and music. This too may be an important means of realizing a Canadian identity in an increasingly interpenetrating world.

In summary, it seems that the system of post-secondary education will have a large demand to meet, and a variety of tasks to fulfil, during the remainder of this century.

The "Conscription" Issue

We are familiar with the argument that education has been oversold, and the statements that young people are "conscripted" into educational institutions and "incarcerated" in "minimum security prisons." Language like this with its roots in emotion rather than reason does little to clarify the situation. In point of fact the period of compulsory schooling in Ontario ends at age sixteen and there is no compulsion on anyone to besiege the admissions offices of colleges and universities every summer and fall. But it is said that students are "conscripted" by parental and social pressures which they find just as strong as legal compulsion, and that people in the universities and colleges add to those pressures by encouraging the students to "serve their full sentence."

There seems to be a widely held belief that there is a "real" education to be had in the "real" world beyond the schools, and that young people could enjoy it freely if they had the courage to break with the culture that keeps them in school. This belief should be judged in the light of the statement that 45 per cent of the nearly half-million Canadians unemployed in November, 1970, were between the ages of fourteen and twenty-four, a large proportion of whom have not completed school. The relationship between lack of education and unemployment is not an invention of academic conspirators, nor is it a new discovery. The hard fact is that the world entering the era of post-industrialism is built on theoretical and abstract knowledge and requires trained intelligence.

Looking at this world as best we can, with its bases in knowledge, innovation and creativity, we cannot bring ourselves to believe that the interests of our youth would be served by cutting back their opportunities for post-secondary education. It follows that we would be neglecting our obligation to youth if we failed to encourage them to pursue their formal education.

Another argument that is raised is that education is continuous over too long a period of time. We would certainly agree that it might be better if more young people interrupted their formal education and then resumed it. This is probably happening to a considerable degree already, though statistics that would establish the extent of this practice are not available. Certainly education has become more a lifetime matter and less a stage of one's early development only.

The Institutional Base

To carry out the tasks enumerated above we start from a basis of more than one hundred post-secondary institutions of various kinds. As we have seen, the more specialized institutions such as teachers' colleges and schools of nursing are being phased, to a large extent, into the more multiform kind of institution. Practically speaking, then, the basis consists in the main of the universities, the CAATs, and Ryerson Polytechnical Institute.

In the past the universities have had sole responsibility for degree work and have taught in the paraprofessional and extension fields in varying measure; they have carried the research load, and taken the lead in the area of social criticism and change. The CAATs, which were deliberately developed to be an alternative to the universities, carry the brunt of technical and technological work for their regular full-time and part-time students and for the retraining of adults, and they do extension work in their communities. Some of the pressures they were designed to meet arose from the numbers graduating from what was called the "four-year stream" in the high schools, a program with a practical rather than an academic emphasis. But with the shift away from streaming towards greater individual choice of program in the schools, this pressure may dissipate. Ryerson, which is *sui generis*, is discussed below.

We propose to look at the entire post-secondary system as one of linked continua in which there must be no dead-end streets.

eople should be able to move to a different area, or to a more
dvanced level, if they develop the interest and demonstrate the
apacity to do so. In other words there should be lateral and
ertical mobility without discriminatory deterrents or the pen-
lty of repetition. Human beings do not sort and sift easily, and
here will always be some who get into the wrong places. The
reater freedom in the secondary schools reduces the "label-
ng" of their graduates and makes it incumbent on the post-
econdary system to increase its flexibility so that any misclassi-
cation can be readily corrected. In other words, we see the
tructure of educational attainment as being inevitably hierar-
hical, but we believe that in the future the upper levels of the
ierarchy and the rewards that attach to achievement should be
ccessible from many routes.

It follows from this that any differentiation between institu-
ions in the system, such as that between CAATs and universi-
es, should be based on a rational assessment of what can be
one best in which kind of institution. For the society of the
uture and for the students of the future we should plan a post-
econdary system which is flexible in its arrangements, which
ermits lateral and vertical mobility to the individual, and
which deploys its resources with a view to service rather than
linging to differentiations based solely on prestige. It is ques-
ionable whether the line should still be drawn so rigidly be-
ween "degree" and "non-degree" work. Already this distinc-
ion is coming to have less reality – some technology courses at
Ryerson are accepted as "degree" work elsewhere, and some
niversity courses given for "degree" credit in the afternoon
are repeated at a college in the evening by the same professor.

The distinction that we see as significant is whether the work
needs to be done by students working with research-oriented
professors or whether it can be accomplished better by students
working with people whose interest and expertise is in teaching
and who do not necessarily pursue research. We shall return to
this distinction.

The universities have a certain planned capacity for expansion, but as we have seen in the previous chapter, the demand
will exceed their planned capacity in a few years' time. If the
universities alone tried to meet this demand they would have to
expand and/or multiply far beyond their planned capacity. Expansion of any university beyond the 20,000-25,000 student

range seems to us to be counter-productive, in that all sense
academic community and prideful identification with an ho
ourable foundation is lost; indeed in some cases this wou
happen long before enrolments of that magnitude we
reached, depending on the university's internal structure an
physical environment. The burgeoning of new colleges an
campuses affiliated to existing universities is a possibility. Hov
ever, if they are geographically distant from the parent institu
tion they will tend to develop independently, and therefore th
possibility merges into the next one, the establishment of seve
al new universities.

Theoretically this would be a logical development from ou
present situation and would build on the sure foundations c
the past. The doubts that we have about this solution are two
fold. They arise partly from indications that "more of th
same" will be too expensive for the economy to handle in th
next few years, and mainly from our belief that a wider diffu
sion of opportunities – geographically, socially and economic
ally, for all ages, by various means – is what the future call
for. On the first point, one idea that dies hard is that excellenc
could be purchased at little expense by establishing "liberal art
colleges" with limited charters that would confine themselv
to undergraduate courses in arts and science and would
without ambitions at other levels. Experience here has show
that the limited charter college idea is unrealistic, if not a con
tradiction in terms. On the second point, if we look ahead fo
ten or twenty years we would hope to see a better distributio
of numbers through the regions of the province and a massiv
decentralization of cultural and economic activity. It therefore
seems logical to use as a basis for long-term educational planning the twenty colleges which with their extra campuses already cover one hundred locations in the province – provided
that the desire, the demand, and the resources exist.

Ideally, the system should be devised so as to reduce to
minimum the social class effects of the inequalities in schoo
achievement, it should promote upward mobility, and it should
facilitate the search for ability that the post-industrial society
requires. Its stratification should match the varying degrees of
attainment of the population, and the test of its eventual success would be the achievement of excellence *in kind* at every
level, combined with the disappearance of socially and economically determined discriminations.

This ideal cannot be achieved overnight, but it should remain in the forefront of our consideration. Recent studies have shown that the choices made very early in a young person's schooling – choices sometimes made with insufficient knowledge or under misleading influences – determine his subsequent career. Massive re-education of parents and teachers is needed. Meanwhile, however, what we can do is to multiply and diversify opportunities at the post-secondary level while at the same time we begin the program of re-education and motivation that is needed.

What follows is one proposal, working with, and from, the existing post-secondary institutions in Ontario.

The Model of Accessible Hierarchy: A New Role for the Colleges

Every region of the province would have centres where degree work in generalist arts and science courses and appropriate first professional degree courses were available. We think that the existing Colleges of Applied Arts and Technology would form the logical base for such centres in most regions. Technical, technological, and extension courses would continue to be given, with the opportunities for part-time students extended as the need dictates. The centres would be community based in the sense that most students would commute to them. They would do no graduate work and their staffs would not be research oriented personnel. The development of degree work would depend on the extent of local demand not being met by any other means. Degree-granting status would be monitored so that there would be no danger of "degree mills" being created: there might be affiliation with universities nearby, or a new over-all degree-granting body might be created as we suggest in the next chapter. Whatever the mechanics, the effect would be to widen the base of generalist education, and to make all the work in the Colleges of Applied Arts and Technology actually and visibly more open-ended.

The universities should continue with their stated plans to expand to a total of about 150,000 undergraduate students by 1975-76, but those universities that have the firmest commitment to advanced and professional work should gradually de-emphasize generalist arts and science as selected CAATs become capable of filling that need, and they should shift more of their resources into the types of work that require highly qualified research-oriented staff.

Old and New Roles for the Universities

1. Undergraduate arts and science "specialist" education of the more intensive kind, described above, for students whose dedication to a branch of learning is so complete that they need no period of orientation. This would preserve a university function which has been well performed by some of the Ontario universities in the past, and would be consistent with a tradition of elitism in our education, but would be a form of controlled and functional elitism, which as we have said earlier would not be exclusive. This specialist education would, of course, be in addition to generalist education at universities which chose to continue the latter. It may be difficult for a while to prevent the division of arts and science work between colleges and universities from reflecting a social class division. We must take it as read that we are not going to achieve an absolutely even distribution by class and/or ability across the institutions, at least not for several years. There will be bumps in the system; but social policy must be to move in the direction of equity and complete equality of opportunity.

2. Post-baccalaureate courses, among which a very important one would be the M.A. program, particularly for graduates of the colleges and of the universities who found some commitment to a subject during their generalist education courses. These M.A. courses would be the junction boxes of the two kinds of arts and science courses, the channels of accessibility to advanced levels of academic work. They would be especially important for teachers, and might be combined with training in pedagogy in Master of Arts in Teaching programs. Doctoral work would continue, perhaps with changed or added emphases.

3. Professional courses of the type demanding considerable involvement with a program of research. In a subsequent chapter we suggest that some of the courses now located in universities should be given more as joint ventures of

universities and colleges. Advanced professional work, and specialization, and the rapidly increasing volume of continuing education, would be done in universities because they require research-oriented personnel as instructors.

4. Research, both on-campus and in affiliated research institutes, which might be either publicly or privately supported.

The model should permit, and indeed encourage, diversity among the various universities and the various CAATs. Where regional considerations are paramount, as in the more sparsely-populated parts of the province, regional groupings of educational resources make sense, and a strong local flavour may be expected to pervade the activities of universities and colleges. Where the population is becoming an almost homogeneous urban mass, the problems to be attacked will be the more general ones of urbanization, and local variants will be less germane. Any special circumstances such as the presence of native Canadian peoples should be reflected in special services. Moreover, the model should encourage some universities to aspire to the highest stature, so that places of a quality to command international recognition are accessible to talented students in Ontario.

Ryerson Polytechnical Institute

The Ryerson Polytechnical Institute has held a unique place in the Ontario system being a pathfinder and a prototype. It is situated at a key pressure point as far as student demand is concerned, and it has established an enviable reputation for the soundness of its programs. We understand that there is a current proposal for Ryerson to grant certain degrees in the near future, becoming, in effect, an additional Ontario university. We see no reason against implementing this proposal as soon as there is sufficient confidence that the Institute can handle the responsibility involved.

Upper-Level Accessibility

We realize that in the model we propose, the universities would retain their responsibility for (or as some would say, their stranglehold on) specialist and advanced studies. If any univer-

71

sity were out of sympathy with the ideas of accessibility tha,
are reflected in this brief, it would be able to erect a barrier t
accessibility at the highest levels by refusing to recognize nev
types of qualification. There is no remedy for this without in
fringing university autonomy, but we regard it as unlikely ir
the highest degree that any Ontario university would take such
an attitude. On the contrary, in order to have true accessibility
in the system, the universities must in the course of time be
prepared to recognize many routes to higher studies: not only
the familiar route direct from high school, but also graduation
from the colleges, and increasingly, we suggest, "units of
experience" in the working world should be accepted as substi-
tutes for classroom credits.

The emphasis – this cannot be said too often – must be on
flexibility from the point of view of the individual student, and
on providing for all students opportunities to move ahead. This
can be done, we are convinced, with no compromising or sacri
ficing the high standards of academic achievement that have
characterized the Ontario system.

CHAPTER 6

THE
ACCESSIBLE
BACCALAUREATE

In this chapter we shall take up the arts/science part of the model, the part concerned with the kinds of education sometimes labelled general/honours, etc., but which we prefer to call generalist and specialist. We have seen in previous chapters that since 1960-61 the enrolment in this sector has risen more rapidly than that in the professional areas and has recently stabilized at around 64 per cent of the total university enrolment. In the CAATs, the popularity of both General Arts and Science and other similar courses, however labelled, is evident. On the face of it, these facts do appear to refute the notion that modern young people are indifferent to learning for its own sake. Some may drift into arts courses as a way of least resistance, but a demand of such magnitude as 64 per cent (at universities) can scarcely be thus accounted for.

Consciously or unconsciously, young people seem to sense where the greatest tasks of the future will lie. Many of these have already been pointed out: the need for scientists in a science-based culture, the need for new and stronger instruments of democratic control of powerful forces, the need to reassert ethical and aesthetic values – in short, the need to redefine and establish the good life in the good society. Thus the traditional disciplines, and the new groupings of disciplines too, are challenged by the problems of the post-industrial society which the citizens of that society must learn to cope with. It is a sound instinct that sends so many into arts and science courses in colleges and universities, whether those courses are viewed as an end in themselves or as a preparation for advanced or professional work. In discussing this component of the model we are at the very heart of the educational process.

We indicated in the last chapter why we believe that the Colleges of Applied Arts and Technology should be gradually given a greater role in meeting the demand for "generalist" education – the main reason being to produce greater flexibility from the student's point of view and to avoid blind alleys in the total system. There are several ways in which this could be done.

Simply to confer upon the CAATs the power to grant degrees, with no attempt to monitor the standard of the degree, would be one way. In spite of the enthusiasm we have heard expressed for this course of action, we cannot help but feel that it is too large a step to take in the time period available – for we must remember that the shortage of places that is expected to develop will become acute in five years' time. The CAATs have achieved a phenomenal development, producing in their first two years some twenty "instant colleges" looking after about 50,000 full and part-time students. There is, as one would expect, unevenness among their staffs in the matters of qualification, experience, and educational philosophy. Realistically, there are some CAATs that are not now able to mount degree courses unadvised and unassisted in the near future, and they know it; but a blanket approval would put them under great local pressure. It would also be unfair to all degree students to encourage variations that would amount to a real letting down of standards.

A second alternative would be to arrange for the development of degree programs in the CAATs to be given by their existing or augmented staffs but with some external academic auspices – say, in affiliation with existing universities. This alternative has much to recommend it. The development of the general arts and science division of a CAAT into a kind of exten-

74

sion department of a sponsoring university would follow the excellent British precedent of the University of London external degrees which at one time had world-wide influence. This arrangement would be viable in centres where university-college relations are close, or where regional considerations point to the desirability of consolidating educational resources. It might or might not lend itself readily to a wider diffusion of opportunities beyond the dozen existing university centres in the province.

A third alternative would be to place the degree work in the CAATs under the control of an over-all body, a new university which could aptly be called the University of Ontario, which would have a strong academic senate drawn from both university and college personnel. If the over-all "University of Ontario" concept were adopted, the geographic outreach of the new development would not be dependent on relationships with any of the existing university centres, but on the other hand it might be more difficult to staff the degree programs when one could not call so readily on the expertise and resources of a nearby university. However we think the idea has merit and deserves consideration.

A fourth alternative, which would also be based on the University of Ontario idea, would involve a new approach to the teaching/learning process which we find very interesting. Much is said and written today about new uses of educational technology and the potential of computers, television, etc., to produce economies in what is admittedly a labour intensive activity, as well as enriching educational programs. We have not been sufficiently impressed by the progress to date in most current applications of educational technology to be confident that any of them will answer the needs of the 1970's and 1980's.

However, a totally new direction in the transmitting of knowledge is dealt with in the UNESCO/I.A.U. publication, *Teaching and Learning,* which forms the basis of experimentation in the British "Open University," and which may signalize a real breakthrough. This whole development is comprehensively explained in Bernard Trotter's preliminary report to the Committee on University Affairs and the Committee of Presidents of Universities of Ontario entitled "Television and Technology in University Teaching." While we are not ourselves in a position to detail the mechanics of how a proposal

like Trotter's would work out, we are greatly impressed
with the proposal and for this reason we are drawing heavily
on his report, as we do below.

The main point of the MacKenzie *et al.* publication, *Teaching and Learning*, is that the teaching/learning process can be
systematized, that is, objectives can be stated, teamwork used
to advantage, results evaluated, and improvements effected. A
useful analogy which we have already mentioned is with developments in the health sciences. The solo practitioner with great
personal authority and close relationships with his patients is
gradually being supplemented by a team approach to the "delivery of health care"; the systematized approach, in its turn,
influences the objectives, methods, and self-evaluation of the
practitioner. It is at least possible that the academic profession
is on the verge of a similar development.

The biggest stumbling block in the way of innovation of the
systems variety is (according to Trotter) not tradition, not
caution, but resources in time and money. The systems approach requires a great deal of time which is just the commodi-
ty that is not to spare in an institution already engaged in the
relentless cycle of undergraduate teaching. Team development
is not an activity which builds up gradually. Demands on time
must be particularly heavy in the initial stages when, in effect,
the faculty members involved are training themselves in a team
development approach. These considerations mean that existing institutions are unlikely to be able, however willing, to
adopt a systems approach to curriculum planning except perhaps on a narrow front, if they are to continue to carry their
ongoing responsibilities effectively. Furthermore, a course development team working within a single institution is unlikely
to have the range of other expensive resources available to it
which, next to time, are required to ensure success.

In proposing the application of the course team development
approach in Ontario, Trotter makes certain assumptions which
include the following:

a) that the degree Bachelor of Arts (general) must represent
   a program (however offered) at least at the level of present work in general arts at Ontario universities and that
   equivalent standards must be established and met;

b) that it will be desirable in the near future to expand the
   opportunities for education at the university level sub-

stantially beyond the capacity of existing universities and without creating new universities on the existing pattern;

c) that it will be desirable to provide these additional opportunities at widely distributed geographic points within the province;

d) that, in order to achieve such a wide distribution of opportunity without loss of quality, it will be necessary to have a highly developed "package" of instructional materials prepared centrally by talented and creative academic teams dedicated to the fullest exploitation of a systematic approach to general education;

e) that there must be a local or regional centre where each student has an institutional home which he shares with fellow students and faculty, and a qualified professoriate to conduct tutorial sessions, to counsel and to assist each student to manage his individual learning experience;

f) that to be successful such an enterprise must be based on a scale of enrolment sufficient to cover the heavy costs of high quality, centrally produced materials and an adequately staffed tutorial service while remaining cost-competitive with existing institutions;

g) that for such a program it is feasible to maintain and possibly improve quality while offering a relatively narrow choice of courses, and that there may be academic advantages in multi-disciplinary courses in which the student's capacity to integrate what he learns in various disciplines is a major instructional objective.

The role of the professor tutor, Trotter says, would be quite different from that of the usual university professor today. He would not be responsible for the basic structure of the course or for preparing lectures or other instructional materials. He would do his teaching within a framework prepared by faculty course teams at the centre. He would, however, retain a great deal of freedom in working with students within the framework of instructional materials provided. It is not suggested that marginally qualified people would receive these appointments; on the contrary they would be full fledged academic faculty with rank and with membership on the academic governing body of the institution, and with sufficient marking assistance and clerical assistance to keep a major proportion of their time available for unscheduled contact with students. The

77

ratio of locally based faculty to students would be approximately one to seventy-five and, without any responsibility for the preparation of teaching materials, faculty would have the opportunity for contact with students at least as close as is normal for general students in conventional circumstances. A process of instruction on this model offers the possibility of genuinely high quality experience to both student and instructor.

In certain courses field-work and/or some limited laboratory experience will be an essential part of the study program. It is assumed, however, that laboratory facilities sufficient for the purposes of the courses offered can be provided at relatively modest cost. (The laboratory package developed by the Open University in Britain costs less than $150 and is designed for use in an ordinary household kitchen.) The challenge to the course development team would be to develop valid, relevant courses in general science and technology for the non-specialist student exploiting mixed media to the full and limiting "live" lab work to the kitchen level.

It is assumed that viewing and listening to such materials would be done on a scheduled basis in each local centre. Technological developments, however, will make it possible in future to have considerable flexibility in playback developments. It is not assumed that distribution of video or audio materials for these courses would depend at all on broadcast or cable distribution facilities. The courses would be designed basically for full-time school-leaving students. Just as the Open University in Britain was established to meet a need for home study opportunity on a part-time basis for adults over 21, the need in Ontario to which this new approach would be directed is the school-leaving population, most of whom will be in the 18-21 age group. By the same token the substantial tutorial support outlined above is designed to meet the special needs of this age group, most of whom will wish to be involved in study on a full-time basis. Clearly, however, the offerings could be made available to part-time students in several ways once the full-time demand has been met.

We have drawn at great length from "Television and Technology in University Teaching" because this particular scheme fits so many of the principles that we believe should govern the development of the post-secondary system. We believe in a

broad-based system of linked continua in the hierarchy of educational institutions, with no dead-end streets for anyone at
any level who discovers the will and interest and possesses the
capacity for work at a higher level. We believe in bringing
opportunities closely and immediately to the attention of those
members of our society who would be unlikely to know about
them or believe in them because of the cultural milieu in which
they grow up. We think that changes in methodology in the
teaching/learning process are permissible, perhaps essential, for
the changing society that is upon us, and that these can be
made without abandoning the quality of the experience. But
the stubborn fact is that experimentation, or even the mere
replication of conventional institutions, would be prohibitively
expensive on the scale that is needed in the very near future.

The course-team development approach described above offers an opportunity to meet the aims of widening access and
retaining quality at relatively modest expense ($1,000 per stu-
dent per year) provided a minimum total enrolment of 20,000
students in the third year is assumed.[1] It would make an intelli-
gent use of teaching resources by relying on non-research-ori-
ented personnel in the colleges, which would remain free of the
high costs associated with research professors, plant and overhead. It would make a place for a new type of academic career,
centred on teaching, and might well call for a special teaching
degree such as the Doctor of Arts already mentioned. The
institutional base that Trotter has defined appears to fit
the Colleges of Applied Arts and Technology which, on other
grounds, as we have argued, should be brought into the spectrum of degree work; and the centrally distributed instructional
material will ensure high quality work from the outset and will
protect the very important feature of upward mobility – assuming at the same time that M.A. programs will be widely available
within the universities as junction boxes for those wishing to
move to advanced studies.

The course-team, composed of highly-qualified academics,

---

[1] Operating and capital costs associated with this proposal are fully explored in
the Appendices to Mr. Trotter's report.

media experts, and curriculum consultants, has potential for every university. But because, in most cases, it demands inter-institutional co-operation on a considerable scale to be cost-competitive, existing institutions are likely to adopt new methods rather slowly. Indeed, there is much wisdom in moving gradually when proven programs in well established institutions are involved. But the need to create new opportunity for large additional numbers of generalist students does offer a spectacular opportunity for radical departure from accustomed practices at minimum risk to existing universities.

We would, then, phrase our fourth alternative as follows: the establishment of an over-all academic body, a fifteenth university called the University of Ontario or some other title that indicates ubiquity rather than locality, chartered to grant generalist degrees by means of a systematized course-team development approach at the centre, with students attending the appropriate regional centres, which we think should normally be a part of the Colleges of Applied Arts and Technology, for viewing and listening to visual and audio materials, for scheduled tutorial sessions and unscheduled contacts with faculty and with other students.

The universities would continue with their expansion as planned, but most of them would gradually de-emphasize the generalist work in arts and science as selected CAATs become capable of filling that need, and would shift more of their resources to specialist and advanced types of work that require highly qualified research-oriented staff.

CHAPTER 7

THE
PROFESSIONAL
LADDER

The principle that all professional and technological education should be part of the regular system of post-secondary education has been reinforced by a number of recent developments in Ontario. To recapitulate: Osgoode Hall has been incorporated into York University, the College of Optometry into the University of Waterloo, the teachers colleges are being moved to the universities, technological institutes have been expanded into Colleges of Applied Arts and Technology, and the recommendations of government committees favour the progressive incorporation of hospital-based schools of technology and nursing into the CAATs. In the last category, the Ontario Committee on the Healing Arts has recommended that educational programs for dental hygienists, nurses, physiotherapists, remedial gymnasts, medical records librarians, health technologists and chiropractors should all be developed in Colleges of Applied Arts and Technology.

The probability is that this trend to integrate rather than to isolate professional education will be sustained rather than reversed in the decades ahead. There are many advantages to the integrated approach. It provides greater opportunity for the student to obtain benefits from his training that can subsequently ease the extension of his educational experience to a new field or to a more advanced level of his original field (lateral or vertical mobility); it gives him a greater choice of careers and reduces the danger of his being trapped in "dead end" specialization or doomed to irreversible obsolescence as a result of technical change; and it minimizes the possibility of the individual student being exploited to meet temporary needs of the market at the expense of a reasonable level of general education. In a world of increasingly complex social problems and interdependent spheres of professional activity, the integrated approach offers more opportunity for interdisciplinary endeavour, which can change in accordance with changing needs.

Not only in teaching but also in fundamental and applied research, it is now and will in the future be increasingly valuable for professional schools of architecture, engineering, health sciences and law to have broad access to faculty in other disciplines. This relationship should facilitate a concerted attack on the complex problems of our society and environment – problems which require diverse and specialized resources not usually found within the professional schools themselves. The institution – presumably, in this case, the university – should provide not only the variety of special resources to cope with the changing problems, but also the *organizational base* from which interdisciplinary endeavours can be mounted with the speed, scope and scale appropriate to the urgency, complexity and magnitude of the problem. If universities can respond to these problems rapidly enough, much responsibility for developmental and innovative research will devolve upon them in the future. The tendency of the past ten years has been for universities to respond to interdisciplinary needs by establishing administrative entities such as institutes or centres. But it is possible that in the next decade a more transient organizational base is required, one which can be more rapidly assembled and dismantled in response to changing needs. With the concomitant instability, the more permanent organizational base of the university at large assumes special significance.

However, the integrated approach to professional and technological education has some possible disadvantages. In the first place, unless those responsible for designing programs have full knowledge of the required levels of skill and judgment, there may be frustration and disappointment for both the student and the employer, and serious damage to the standards of public service. Secondly, if the professional or technological aspects of the programs are too deeply submerged in general education, the student may lose the sense of relevance that inspires his commitment to learning.

Counter measures to offset these potential dangers can and should be taken. It would be wise to have provincial advisory boards, which include in their membership educators, employers, members of the professions concerned, and representatives of the public, to establish minimum technological and professional standards for programs, leaving the educational treatment of these programs to the institutions concerned. Any such advisory board must try to ensure that the goals of professional education are those assigned by society as a whole, not those of the profession alone, or educators, or employers. The danger of lack of relevance could be countered by developing diverse forms of interaction between the educational system and the outside world, and in particular by maintaining field work or clinical experience as a significant part of professional or technological education. This minimizes the disparity between the "theoretical" world of education and the "real" world of practice, and may assist in conditioning both worlds to change.

Although we recognize the desirability of the general trend towards integrated programs, we should not exclude the possibility of singular professional training institutions emerging in engineering science and technology or in social and health affairs. The cluster of professions and technologies involved in such a development might be closely related to a specific mission; but the educational and research base should be broad, as has been the case, for example at M.I.T. or Cal. Tech. Ontario should be prepared to accommodate such a development within the post-secondary educational system, with status equivalent to that of a chartered university. But it would be better still for such an institution to emerge as a unique national resource.

Respective Roles of Colleges and Universities

In the existing post-secondary educational system there are two alternatives (apart from the single-purpose professional school) for the location of professional and technological programs: Colleges of Applied Arts and Technology, or universities. Arguments can usually be found in the case of any individual professional program to favour its location in either division of the system. Collectively, however, it is difficult to deny the desirability of locating some professional and technological programs in each type of institution. The most formidable barrier to the development of professional programs in CAATs rather than universities seems to be the matter of prestige, which is of great concern to the parents of students and to the professional group concerned. The barrier of prestige might be overcome in several ways: allowing the passage of time to prove the quality of CAAT programs and to earn genuine acceptance from parents, employers, and professional associations; providing academic degrees for programs which would satisfy students, parents, and professions anxious to have the traditional symbols of a completed university education; and, finally, the formal establishment of channels for lateral and vertical mobility for graduates of the CAATs without discriminatory deterrents or the penalty of repetition.

It is most important for the students who complete these programs to have the assurance that their educational experience will be recognized should they wish to transfer into another professional program at a later stage, or should they wish to proceed to a more advanced stage of education in their own profession. The problem of recognition is real, since in most cases there will not be any direct equivalence of courses of study if the programs of universities and CAATs faithfully reflect distinctive educational objectives. The problem may, however, be minimized if more weight can be given to the academic *potential* of the applicants for advanced work, and greater latitude allowed in the courses of study to be selected, so as to permit the rectification of previous deficiencies.

In selecting the site for a specific educational program, two of the most important criteria are the educational objectives and the degree of involvement of the program with the process of research. The primary objective of professional and technological programs in the CAATs should be the achievement of an effective standard of technical performance. Programs in the universities should be aimed at preparing individuals for responsibilities involving judgment in professional practice requir-

84

ing not only the possession of knowledge and skills but also the
ability to apply them to the solution of unfamiliar problems.
Programs in both institutional settings require significant practical experience, but in the one case the perfection of technique
is of primary importance, whereas in the other, problem-solving ability deploying techniques, information, and the skills of
other personnel is paramount. The generalizations stated are a
matter of emphasis; obviously there is no sharp dividing line
between the type of program which might be managed effectively in a CAAT and that in a university.

A second consideration is that the CAATs should be concerned almost exclusively with the transmission of knowledge,
whereas the universities must in addition give significant emphasis to the advancement of knowledge. The location of a
professional program, therefore, will be strongly influenced by
the importance of related research activity, and this, of course,
affects the proportion of staff time available for teaching and
the special facilities and operating costs of the program.

It follows, then, that professional programs which have as
their objective the development of the ability to handle abstract
concepts and which may benefit from intimate relationship between educational and research activity, should continue to be
based in the universities. Those which have more practical
objectives, particularly the training of technologists, technicians
and professional assistants, should be in the CAATs. While basic
(first degree) professional programs could be in either type of
institution, advanced professional work will probably, for the
most part, be carried out in the universities, although the possibility of specific technically oriented advanced level programs
in the colleges should not be excluded.

The greatest benefits of the differentiation of roles can only
be achieved if the resources of CAATs and universities which are
in close geographic proximity are functionally pooled. This
would involve making courses and other types of professional
experience available to the students of either institution; having
successive stages of primary educational experience in both institutions; having advanced level programs at either institution
for graduates of both; deploying the support services such as
library, audiovisual resources and exhibits for the use of either
institution, and, finally, joint use of field work or experimental
and clinical facilities by students in both groups. The joint use

of experimental and clinical facilities is particularly important since, in relation to professional tasks, this provides for teamwork among professional and technological groups with common missions. Perhaps the most important joint enterprise should be the planning of future developments; the beneficial results from a high level of co-operation achieved locally cannot be expected to be duplicated by policies legislated centrally.

The entire development should be viewed as a *regional educational resource centre* with primary emphasis on the post-secondary programs of formal education of the colleges and universities, but also vitally concerned with continuing education. The primary aim should not exclude making available support services and special educational opportunities for gifted students in the secondary school system if greater demand for advanced elective experience occurs. The mobility of students will be greatly facilitated, and considerable economies may be realized, if there is a geographic linkage between colleges and universities engaged in work at different levels in the professional fields of social service, engineering and health. These clutches of professions should share the use of resources, including personnel; they should also share certain educational experiences. But the distinctive objectives of professional education, which are different for the colleges and the universities, should be maintained.

Different routes to the more advanced levels of professional education should also be recognized. Besides the route which we now consider to be the norm, involving university experience, there should be a route through the CAATs, as previously noted, and indeed, a third route through demonstrated competence in practical or field experience. This will require a broadening of admissions criteria to professional programs to recognize performance of a non-scholarly nature. With students from diverse backgrounds it would be necessary to offer more options in the curriculum in order to rectify deficiencies in theoretical knowledge associated with previous educational or work experience. Professional status in engineering can be conferred through the APEO examinations on individuals who lack a degree from an accredited school of engineering, but the success rate in the examinations is extremely low, only 3 per cent in 1970.

Greater educational opportunity for people at various stages in their lives would be provided by having different entry points into the system of any profession – from an educational base, a technological base, or a base of working experience. The routes of entry from working experience and from a technological career offer perhaps the best mechanism for circumventing the obstacles to advancement up the professional ladder for those talented individuals whose career potential has been limited by the environment of early life or by incompatibility with the standard educational system. There is a real danger, however, that the availability of greater opportunities for advancement will result in the conversion of excellent technicians into second-rate professionals because of the desire for status. However, rather than limiting opportunity, it seems preferable to search for ways to enhance social appreciation of the essential need for a spectrum of complementary roles and skills.

Duration of Professional Education

With few exceptions the trend over the past decades has been to lengthen the duration of formal full-time post-secondary professional education. The progressive lengthening may be explained in part by the rapid growth of the information base relevant to the profession and the educators' faithful adherence to the building block concept of education. The trend to specialization has been most striking in medicine where the interval between high school graduation and the completion of specialty training ranges from ten to fourteen years. However, the demand for specialized professional qualifications may be expected to stimulate the growth of academically supervised specialty training programs in other professions such as engineering, law, business, education, and social and environmental studies.

In many professions, particularly those which are less well established and academically secure, there is a tendency to stiffen admission requirements and press for longer educational programs in the belief that the length of the program can be correlated with the prestige of the profession. This results in the exclusion of many students who might otherwise be academically and financially able to cope with the program, and in increased cost to society both during the person's education and after his qualification to practise. The provincial advisory boards mentioned earlier would be the appropriate means of checking unnecessary prolongation of programs.

Although the prolongation of training has been the general trend, a few examples exist of a reversal of that trend. By co-ordinating undergraduate clinical experience, internship and residency training, one full year has been eliminated from the postgraduate specialty training in medicine. One Ontario medical school has condensed the conventional four year curriculum into three academic years, while another is exploring the abbreviation of premedical experience to one year after Grade 13.

We would argue that many professional programs might benefit from a *shortening* of the period of continuous formal full-time study and from an abandonment of the lock-step schedule, so that students might proceed at their own pace. Furthermore, if the objectives of training can be clearly defined and more effective assessment procedures introduced, it is difficult to see why some advanced professional training might not be taken in practice on a part-time basis over a longer time interval without the necessity for prolonged full-time training. To encourage this trend, the system of financing professional training should be geared more to the results of the process than to the number of years of training, and should not discourage part-time or co-operative approaches to advanced levels of qualification.

One obvious way to shorten professional training would be to eliminate the general educational component as well as any aspects which cannot be identified as immediately relevant to the professional role. This temptation must be resisted because of the danger of producing technologists or dead-end specialists without potential for renewal, substitution, or vertical mobility.

A prolonged, uninterrupted educational experience may be too expensive for the student; it may blunt his motivation to learn; and it may result in his finding himself unable to adapt his skills readily to the circumstances of a working role. Furthermore, the rapid growth of knowledge and technique will render obsolete a substantial portion of the content of this educational experience within a few years of his entry into practice. It seems desirable to shorten the initial period of continuous professional education and to defer highly specialized training to a subsequent stage, or else to provide a base subsequently supplemented by a structured approach to continuing education in the subject areas of greatest relevance. It remains to be demonstrated whether professional service can be improved by giving professionals intermittent rather than continuous formal education.

Continuing Education and Requalification

Few professionals can be prepared for a lifetime of effective practice on the basis of initial training alone, and in all professions more vigorous support for regular renewal is needed, to be achieved through financial incentives, periodic re-licensing or other mechanisms. The process of continuing education should improve the standard of professional practice, and at the same time make professions responsive to an accelerating pace of change in the goals, values and technology of society. The ideal would be to bring continuing education to the practitioner in actual problem-solving situations of professional practice. This implies a reaching out beyond the walls of the university and will involve imaginative applications of communications and self-learning techniques as well as a network of tutorial resources, possibly structured along the lines of the "University of Ontario" model.

If the responsibility for lifelong continuing education for the professions in a "catchment" area were assumed by the university or CAAT, the teaching load of the institution would be increased to an extent that does not seem to have been generally realized, and a predictable means of financing would be required which is not currently available. The Committee on the Healing Arts recommended[1] that every physician be required to provide evidence of a satisfactory level of competence every five years and that Ontario faculties of medicine develop a program which presumably would include both education and evaluation. If for each million of population in the region served by a medical school, approximately 1,000 physicians received the equivalent of one year of full-time education every five years, the result would be a teaching load equivalent to 200

---

[1] *Report of the Committee on the Healing Arts*, Vol. II, p. 81.

full-time medical students per year. (The 1970 formula equivalent would be greater than $1,700,000.)

In a similar vein, the 1970 study of engineering education in Ontario[2] recommends periodic requalification requiring successful completion of courses perhaps every five years. The magnitude of this educational task for schools of engineering may be appreciated if one notes that in 1969-70 about 4,000 graduate engineers would require requalification in Ontario, as compared with a total full-time equivalent undergraduate enrolment of 8,226. Moreover, the distribution of the teaching load would likely be uneven; and if a strictly regional approach to the problem were taken, its effectiveness might be limited by reason of the restricted areas of special competence available in each school.

Since the benefits of continuing education should be measured in terms of the quality, effectiveness and economy of the professional services rendered, it would be justifiable to look to the "industry" concerned, the employer, to underwrite the educational costs. In the case of self-employed professionals some other arrangement would be necessary. The high cost of effective continuing education and periodic retraining stems in part from the need to tailor the learning situation to individual students' needs – unlike initial professional training where all the students have similar backgrounds and are at approximately the same stage of learning and where larger group instruction may be appropriate. The high cost of retraining also reflects the need to extend the program into the community, in person or by communications devices, as an extramural curriculum with effective dialogue between instructor and student, rather than withdrawing useful persons from practice for substantial periods of time.

Influence of Professional Associations

Rigidity, traditionalism and resistance to change in professional education are usually attributed by educational critics to the influence of the organized professional associations. While this

[2] P. A. Lapp, et al., Ring of Iron: A Study of Engineering Education in Ontario. (Toronto, CPUO.), 1970.

charge had substance a decade ago, the influence of these associations has been greatly reduced in most professions. At the present time, in some professions at least, the forces of resistance to change in the curriculum appear to be stronger *in the schools and universities themselves* than in the professional associations. This inertia results from a failure to recognize the problems of a changing society and the stubborn insistence on scholastic achievement at the expense of professional relevance.

Many of the professional associations retain ultimate authority for the standard of education through the power of licensure, but even this power is delegated by the province, and may be revoked if it is not exercised in the public interest. The public interest might be better served if professional licensing and certifying bodies included lay representation, as was recommended for the health professions by the Ontario Committee on the Healing Arts. An added provision should be a regular turnover of both educational and lay representatives on these boards to ensure fresh viewpoints.

Although professional education is often branded as inflexible, outdated and irrelevant, this image may be misleading. In fact, during the past few years, the changes in educational methods and upheavals in curriculum organization in certain schools of architecture, engineering, law and medicine are among the most dramatic in the Ontario university system and reflect a new emphasis on relevance to changing social conditions. Admittedly this is very recent history and in most cases the changes may have been long overdue. Furthermore, the reforms are not uniform for all the professional schools in the province, nor is it desirable that they should be, since in many cases the innovations are experimental and require evaluation before they are widely applied.

In the professional fields the opportunity to overcome academic insularity is great. Academic and field experience may be interspersed by using real life situations for laboratory or practical experience, and by making summer employment an academically supervised, educational experience during which the primary objective is to learn, not to earn. Such contacts with the actual situations of professional practice, coming early in the course of the educational program, should ensure a more positive motivation on the part of the students, a greater sense of relevance, and a more informed base for the subsequent choice of careers. On the other hand, field experience will bring none of these benefits if the students are exploited as cheap labour and not given meaningful responsibilities.

Professional associations are frequently accused of promoting restrictive or exclusive practices in their respective educational programs. As already noted, there does seem to be validity to the charge that some professions as a matter of prestige press relentlessly for "upgrading" to degree level by increasing the stringency of admission requirements or by extending the duration of training.

There is less evidence that the professions are guilty of a conspiracy to restrict enrolment in professional programs to protect their employment monopoly. Indeed, in medicine (the example most frequently cited), the organized profession has been very active in encouraging the establishment of new schools and the expansion of existing programs. Resistance to the expansion of programs has come in part from educators who have been concerned with possible sacrifices of quality to quantity and the shortage of qualified faculty, and in part from government which recoils in horror from the large expenditures involved.

In the interests of providing the maximum educational opportunity for Ontario citizens, particularly in fields such as medicine and dentistry where there is a large surplus of qualified applicants, we suggest that it would now seem preferable to expand the enrolment in our university system, rather than continuing to rely on the embarrassingly large migration from other provinces and countries which can ill afford to lose highly trained personnel.

Manpower Production and the Proliferation of Professions

Official provincial policy respecting accessibility of post-secondary education might be described as "open door" in general, but not with respect to professional programs where in some instances there are far more qualified applicants than places available. Two rather different approaches to the numbers in professional courses present themselves. The first, which seems to enjoy favour in some professions, for example, education, is based on predictions of manpower needs. These predictions are subject to serious miscalculations, since they usually represent extrapolations from past experience and do not take into account changes in technology, social needs, or migration. Tight coupling of professional production to manpower forecasts is particularly dangerous for the longer educational programs in which the interval between the recognition of a miscalculation and the results of correcting it may be five to eight years. Furthermore, a model of the market which relies on the control of production in Ontario universities overlooks the portability of professional credentials and the substantial fluctuations in immigration and emigration which are beyond provincial influences in most professions and currently not regulated in relation to national objectives.

An alternative approach is the "open" policy of making opportunities as far as possible available to all those with adequate academic qualifications who are interested. Enrolment in these circumstances would be strongly influenced by student demand and a greater incentive might be required to encourage students to enter understaffed fields. For expensive programs such as medicine and dentistry, this would be a costly approach if production exceeded estimates of need, and it would not be feasible to allow wide fluctuations in enrolment from year to year. The open approach has the merit of preserving individual opportunity, and it has the disadvantages of substantial cost to the province and possible disappointment for the trainee if he does not find the employment of his choice after graduation. A by-product of the open approach is the creation of a reservoir of talent which might be applied to unanticipated needs, or, indeed, would be more likely to generate new avenues of development.

The latter "entrepreneurial potentiality" is particularly strong for professions such as engineering and law. For example, more than half of all professional engineers take on a management role within fifteen years of graduation. In aiding the development of technologically intensive industry and in initiating new forms of interprofessional services, we should expect increased leadership from the professionally educated.

There is little evidence to suggest that automation and its concomitants will decrease opportunities for professional service or that the availability of paraprofessional services will displace professional roles. Rather, as the interactive character of the post-industrial society becomes more complex, the roles

93

of professional persons will continually be recast. In this sense
professional education in the future has the responsibility tc
develop a stronger capacity to adapt to the changing social anc
industrial context, and hence requires a significant measure of
freedom to develop. As noted in the opening chapter, the possibilities of serious shortages of people who can handle the levels
of increased complexity of knowledge are great.

While maximum freedom of opportunity for professional education is a desirable long-term goal, a more cautious approach
is necessary in regard to the establishment of new professions
and technologies until the need for them is thoroughly documented. The unplanned proliferation of professions, and exces-
sive specialization within professions, can lead to fragmenta-
tion and maldistribution of services, increased costs, and counter-productive rivalry and competition.

It would appear, therefore, that *the long-term trend in professional education should be towards an open door policy*, including
frequent re-education for practitioners and opportunities for
up-grading from the lower levels; and that all the consequences
should be recognized. Society would be ill-served if an increase
in numbers educated in the professions were to vitiate the quality of the educational process, and, therefore, that of the professional services rendered.

It is of paramount importance in these matters to place the
public interest foremost. We are therefore led to suggest an
even broader role for the public regulatory boards which have
already been mentioned in connection with licensure and certification. Such boards, including spokesmen for the professions,
educators, employers, and the public should review the supply
of manpower, the upgrading of educational programs and the
recognition of new fields. Professional services are too important to be left to professionals alone.

CHAPTER 8

THE
HIGHEST
LEARNING

It seemed evident to us that the progress of human knowledge in this century has achieved such proportions, has expanded so enormously, has moved into such previously unknown and unimagined areas as well as vastly modifying the already substantial burden of human learning received from the past, that it can be continued and stimulated further, absorbed and made intelligible, only if it is organized.[1]

The increase in the growth of knowledge is, to a significant degree, the result of research undertaken by university scholars. In Canada, as elsewhere, the continuation of this growth is a vital element in our innovative capacity and our national identification. If this growth is to continue as part of Canada's role

---

[1]*Graduate Studies in the University of Toronto*, Report of the President's Committee on the School of Graduate Studies (Toronto: University of Toronto Press, 1965), p. 14.

in the post-industrial world, three conditions must prevail
graduate work must be improved in quality, it must be coordinated within and among universities, and it must be continually assessed in terms of provincial and national needs, particularly in terms of a viable national science policy.

The first two conditions – improvement and co-ordination –
have been for some time the concern of the Ontario Council or
Graduate Studies whose membership includes the graduate
deans in the Ontario universities. In 1966 the Spinks Commission recommended that rational forward planning in graduate
studies be strengthened, and in particular that steps be taken "to
ensure co-operation and co-ordination between the universities
in the field of graduate studies and research, with a view both to
develop excellence and to economize resources," and "to develop a number of centres of excellence in the universities of Ontario, which might achieve an international respect and renown."[2]
The Spinks Commission recognized that high standards of quality in graduate programs require substantial government financial support, and that such support will increasingly depend on
evidence of co-ordination and economy in its use.

Following the release of the Spinks Report the Ontario
Council on Graduate Studies established its Appraisals Committee, and each university agreed to submit all new graduate
programs to the Appraisals Committee for a judgment on
their academic quality before final approval by the university.
Since its inauguration nearly four years ago, the Appraisals
Committee has gained the confidence of the academic community of Ontario.

The other concern of the Council is with the orderly development of graduate studies in the Province, which of course
involves co-operation and co-ordination. With the degree of
autonomy enjoyed by the universities of Ontario, each institution has had the power to initiate graduate programs without
necessarily considering whether similar programs were available in other institutions. On the Council's recommendation, the

---

[2] *Report* to the Committee on University Affairs and the Committee of Presidents of Provincially Assisted Universities of Ontario of the Commission to
Study the Development of Graduate Programmes in Ontario Universities,
1966, p. 83.

Committee of Presidents convened a meeting in May 1968 of
the heads of departments in all disciplines. As a result, a number of discipline committees were set up to formulate methods
of co-operation and co-ordination in graduate programs.

The Council on Graduate Studies recognized that these aims
could only be achieved through the initiatives taken by discipline committees. It therefore organized its Advisory Committee
on Academic Planning to stimulate and support these initiatives,
and its recommendations about possible approaches to co-ordination have been referred back to the senates of the universities. The result of all this unhurried (not to say sluggish) and
widespread discussion in the halls of academic democracy is a
mechanism that may prove to be of crucial value and useful-
ness in the sensitive area of Discipline Assessment, which involves consideration of total provincial needs and resources.
There may, for example, be special facilities such as personnel,
library, equipment, or even geographic circumstances, which
make a particular university a natural choice for the development of some aspect of a discipline. It may be clear that some
area of society is short of highly qualified personnel, or is
overstocked with them. In either case such information is
weighed in making recommendations for further development.
Again, the existence of a moribund program at one university
is noted in considering the aspirations at another. The newly-
published report of the Lapp Commission is a prototype of
such assessment. One difficulty is that in its present form, assessment is a time-consuming procedure, and if it is to succeed
it must operate faster than present plans envisage.

We have devoted a good deal of emphasis to the development of program appraisal and discipline assessment in Ontario because we believe that this development is a step of paramount importance to the post-secondary system for the years
ahead. With the trends that we have been describing to part-
time study, to interrupted formal education, to co-ordination
of programs with other post-secondary institutions, to increased participation of students in curriculum planning; with
the probability of the Master's degree developing as an important bridge from college-level to advanced-level work; with the
shift from departmental empires to interdisciplinary centres,
perhaps to be succeeded by still more fluid and impermanent
structures, it is fortunate that the universities have already or-

ganized mechanisms for planning and analysis on a province-wide scale under academic control. Graduate studies is the logical place to start because there can be little doubt that the need for rationalization is greatest at this level. Frequently, however, such planning will have effects on undergraduate offerings. Looking ahead, we can visualize a form of discipline assessment that would embrace the whole post-secondary field, and we can hope that the experience we have gained at the graduate level will be useful and effective when it is called for in a broader sphere.

One of the obstacles to rational planning is the concept of absolute university autonomy. In contrast to the freedom of the individual member of the university to dissent, to criticize, to investigate the unknown (which is basic), institutional autonomy can and must be considerably compromised. Absolute autonomy exists today only in the rhetoric of convocation platforms; public financing involves public service and public accountability. However, having recognized the fact, the universities still have room to manoeuvre if they can agree among themselves on measures of sensible cooperation and if they will establish and support the necessary machinery to implement them. If government bodies undertake to rationalize graduate programs, the tendency will be to stress those that appear to meet specific, visible needs in fields such as health, transportation, conservation and so on, and the importance of non-vocational programs will diminish. Only by undertaking rational planning themselves – ceding some autonomy to their peer-group – can the universities hope to preserve their own scale of values.

Because it is expensive, graduate work is a prime target for the economiser's axe, as current events make clear. We hope that the retrenchment will be short-lived. If in the future the universities as the centres of knowledge and innovation have a key role to play, obviously the quality and type of their work at the highest levels will be of crucial importance. It may well be that in the post-industrial society the growth of knowledge and the complexity of our technology with its attendant problems will create a demand for a flow of graduates at the masters and Ph.D. levels equivalent to that at the baccalaureate level in the industrial society. The post-secondary system, which may have to meet demands on that scale, should not be hobbled by reaon of a seeming over-production at this point in time.

Looking towards the 1980's, we can prophesy with some certainty that a crucial element in the future development of graduate studies is *the adaptability of graduate instruction to different fields of activity rather than one specific field.* For the past decade or so graduate schools have been preoccupied with the production of highly trained specialists to meet the demands for highly skilled manpower of an expanding industrial society. As industrial expansion has slowed in the past year or two some graduates thus prepared have encountered difficulty in finding employment suited to their particular skills. We are aware that the outlook for jobs directly related to a particular field of study may at times be very uncertain, and we must expect discrepancies between the supply of and demand for human resources. It is long-term factors, not short-run shifts in market demand or in student preferences, that should guide the development of graduate programs.

We must remember that the growth in the graduate student intake in Ontario universities in the past decade in large part has been due to the sharp demand for faculty in our greatly expanded university community. Without this substantial increase in the growth of graduate schools, the expansion would have been much slower. Indeed, in order to meet this demand our universities were forced to seek qualified faculty from other countries, notably the United States and Britain. Now that this type of demand is lessening we must consider the long term factors which will shape the demand for graduate students. As the Committee on University Affairs pointed out in its latest report, "Canada, through the Federal Government and its various agencies, is now in the course of a major review of national science policy. It seems reasonable to anticipate that the results of this will become evident in government policy before the end of 1971. If, as seems fairly probable, Canada should determine to take a more aggressive line in research and development with respect to urban development, transportation, housing, the North and so forth, we could possibly find ourselves again endeavouring to force the expansion of graduate enrolment."[3]

---

[3] *Report of the Committee on University Affairs of Ontario 1969-70,* p. 18.

Another long term factor which cannot be overlooked in the development of graduate programs is the effort which universities must exert in helping our country to meet its international obligation to supply highly skilled manpower for the developing nations. We cannot overlook the fact that the movement of graduate students has been to Canada's advantage. To quote the Committee on University Affairs once again: "In most countries today, outstanding graduate students are urged to travel to broaden perspectives and to work with leading scholars in chosen fields of study. For Canada particularly, this was pretty much a one-way street until recently. Most Canadian choosing to do graduate study did it in the USA. or in Britain (at the expense of taxpayers in those countries). Some returned. Until the mid-60's very few foreign graduate students came to Canada. But since that time the situation has altered considerably. It must be regarded as appropriate that we should reciprocate for the benefits Canadians have enjoyed for many years in other jurisdictions. And, selfishly, it was acknowledged that the graduate school was a good device for encouraging the immigration of high level manpower."[4]

It is our belief that, ideally, all those in our society who have the ability, capacity and motivation necessary for any level of education should be given the opportunity of reaching that level. This is an "open door" policy which is not capable of implementation in the short run because we have not as yet sufficient knowledge of the meaning of ability or capacity, or of the dynamics of the relationship between economic, social and psychological factors on the one hand and motivation on the other. *We believe, nevertheless, that there should be a continuing thrust in our educational policies towards an "open door" policy at all levels.*

It is likely that we have at this present juncture, as John Porter has said, "a problem of over-specialization rather than over-production. In that case our educational planning is at fault because we place too great an emphasis on specific discipline content rather than on content common to all disciplines." He goes on to say that "the post-industrial society is one of accelerated rates of change. Therefore, those who leave

---

[4] *Ibid.*

our universities should have skills that are flexible in a rapidly changing world."[5] However, our graduate schools continue to produce highly trained specialists in very narrow fields, with the result that the graduates seek positions in a very narrow area of competence, thereby severely limiting their choice of a job. Part of the difficulty, of course, stems from the current policy of economic restraints which has led to cutbacks in appropriations for research which these graduates are qualified to undertake. But it is obvious that many of them have great difficulty in adapting themselves to a different type of activity.

If it is true, as Porter suggests, that our graduates' problem is over-specialization, we should ask if our graduate schools are producing the right product. The Ph.D. may be out of date. Professor Hall of McMaster University has made this point very well: "The knowledge worker in the post-industrial age operates quite differently from his counterpart in the industrial age. The spectrum of knowledge that he possesses at any given time is constantly changing. Thus, such an individual may be doing one thing for a few years but because of changes in his field, is soon involved in another type of activity. Consequently, such an individual needs to be adaptable, versatile and have the basic skills and motivation to continually learn new ways of doing things and applying this information. A premium is placed on skills rather than on the specialized knowledge that he may possess at any given time."[6]

An attack on this problem will require a careful examination of present graduate curricula and a willingness to experiment with "curricula based on the principle of stating questions, organizing knowledge and methods of attacking problems as opposed to the assimilation of specific bodies of knowledge".[7] The representatives of one discipline, Chemistry, have stated the problem and a possible solution as follows: "The rapid growth of science and technology has created even greater de-

---

[5] John Porter, "Post-Industrialism, Post Nationalism and Post-Secondary Education" (paper for the National Seminar on the Costs of Post-Secondary Education, Institute of Public Administration of Canada, June, 1970), pp. 27-8.
[6] *Globe and Mail*, June 2, 1970.
[7] J. R. Gass, "Equality, Quantity and Quality in Education," *OECD Observer*, June 1969, p. 15.

mands for adaptability over both the short-term and the long-term. Added breadth would lead not only to a greater capability for careers in chemical sciences, but also to greater overall flexibility."[8]

We should be experimenting with alternative curricula, not only to create greater market substitutability of graduates, but also to provide society with adaptable and versatile individuals who can see beyond the confines of a particular discipline to the problems facing society at large. The emerging post-industrial society will need substantial numbers of such people. We must ask if the present graduate curriculum is geared to the provision of adaptable individuals.

Cragg and Nestman have proposed a kind of "troika" system of Ph.D. programs.[9] This proposal is intended to provide for the kind of adaptable graduates we have mentioned, to fill the need for a continuing supply of university faculty, and to produce people with substantial research training. In Law's words this restructured Ph.D. program would:

1. Train some Ph.D.'s for undergraduate teaching – this section would not be heavily research oriented.
2. Train a second group in in-depth research; both research and course work would be broader than the present Ph.D. programs.
3. Train the third group of Ph.D. candidates around a core of courses with less specialization and more flexibility; out of this type of program would come leadership to overcome special technological problems such as pollution, planning for innovation, and industrial management . . .

(The first part, the doctorate for undergraduate teaching, might be the Doctor of Arts degree that was referred to earlier.)

The problem of change in the graduate curriculum can be stated in another way. It seems likely that the post-industrial society will require a new type of generalist, one who has not

[8]Preliminary Report, *International Conference on Education in Chemistry*, Division of Chemical Education, American Chemical Association, July, 1970, p. 32.
[9]Harriet Law, "Strong Medicine for Scientists Facing a Plethora of Ph.D.'s" *Canadian University & College*, Vol. 5, No. 10, Oct., 1970, p. 31.

only mastered a basic core of knowledge but also has enough adaptability and scholarly commitment to use that knowledge in a new way in his search for an understanding of, and solution to, problems. His search may *require* the mastery of a body of specialized knowledge, in which case he would assume for this purpose the role of a specialist, focusing his abilities and skills on a limited problem area. His basic training would enable him to assume the duties of a teacher; if he wished to engage in research he would need to add to his basic familiarity with his field by concentrating on a special area. The new generalist could thus move from teaching to research – from a purely teaching role to a concentration on a particular research problem – and back to teaching. He would not at any stage become so lost in the realm of specialization that he found himself out of touch with basic developments.

It has been generally accepted that research is a basic ingredient of graduate study – research being understood as systematic study and investigation in some field of knowledge, undertaken to establish facts or principles, whether or not there is any obvious "payoff" in terms of a specific need to be met. This view of research as a systematic process, however, tends to mask the fact that nearly all that is essential to the academic life of the university from work at the most elementary to the most advanced level is a kind of research. Undergraduates, though they may discover nothing new, should be engaged in research rather than being taught, that is to say, they should be active participants in a process of discovery, not passive spectators. Faculty members, though they too may discover nothing new, should be active enquirers and not mechanical repeaters. In this sense, "research" becomes a kind of shorthand description of what traditionally has been regarded as the scholarly vocation: the individual and common pursuit of knowledge. An implication of this view is that teaching itself is not confined to the dissemination of knowledge. It is a voyage of discovery which may be creative. If teaching is to be stimulating for teacher as well as student, it requires time for preparation and reflection; in this reflective process new ideas and fresh approaches to subject matter may emerge. Teaching thus is creative, providing an atmosphere for both teacher and student that is intellectually stimulating and pregnant with new ideas for systematic research.

103

In the following chapter we shall consider research in the sense of a nationally important activity, standing in its own right, as it were. Here it is appropriate to speak of research in particular relation to the training of graduate students, and we make this comment: it would be a disservice to the Canada and the Canadians of the future if fundamental research were neglected because of scarce funds and an over-emphasis on applied research. Joseph Ben-David has pointed out that "obvious leads to discoveries which would revolutionize broad fields of knowledge would be passed over for minor technological solutions because there would be no professional scientists to pursue leads of merely theoretical significance. In the long run this would be economically inefficient. Important theoretical advances usually have great indirect practical potentialities which can be exploited if there are entrepreneurs bringing them to the attention of technologists and others who may be concerned. But technological solutions, even if they have great potentialities for generalization, will hardly reach that stage in the absence of professional scientists whose job is to theorize and generalize."[10]

Ben-David sees the solution to this problem lying in a re-evaluation of the relationship between fundamental and applied research. "The relationship between fundamental and applied research should not be visualized as a series of separate links between certain fundamental discoveries and their 'applications'. Rather, practical uses of science should be conceived as the result of chance interactions between fundamental discoveries on the one hand and practical interests on the other, which can occur in an infinite variety of ways. The purpose of policy should, therefore, be to influence the likelihood of these chance occurrences by increasing the density of both kinds of activities and the velocity of the circulation of ideas and problems from both areas of activity in spaces which ensure interaction. Increasing the density is a matter of investment, velocity is the result of entrepreneurship, and creating the properly enclosed spaces is a task for organization."[11]

---

[10]Joseph Ben-David, *Fundamental Research and the Universities* (Paris: OECD, 1968), p. 60.
[11]*Ibid.*

We suggest that investment is a task for federal, provincial, and private granting bodies. Entrepreneurship in science and social science policy might be a task for an expanded Science Council, or the Canada Council. Organization is a task for the universities. Needless to say, these tasks require the closest co-operation of all three groups.

CHAPTER 9

THE
EXTENSION
OF
KNOWLEDGE

The word "research" and its synonyms are used in many different senses, and it will be worthwhile to glance back at what has already been mentioned under the name of research before going on to explain the particular sense in which we shall use the word in this chapter.

We mentioned research earlier as one of the services performed for society by universities, as well as being done in research institutes and industrial laboratories, and we spoke of a distinction between pure and applied research. (Semantic difficulties in this area are such that it can be said quite seriously that "pure" is a dirty word nowadays.) We have spoken of research as one of the professor's occupations and we suggested that the elevation of research (specifically of *published* research) to be the main or sole criterion for advancement has resulted in much low-quality publication and in an unfair depreciation of the value of good teaching. In the chapter on professional education, research was tied in to the instruction of those at the more advanced levels whose programs have as their objectives abstract learning and problem-solving abilities. In the last chapter it was spoken of as what used to be called scholarly vocation, the individual's voyage of discovery at any level; and the suggestion was made that the universities should provide the environment for many contacts between fundamental researchers and those who deal with practical problems, on the grounds that chance interactions between such people are responsible for scientific and technological advances.

Since science and technology are the basis of post-industrial society, advancement and innovation in those fields acquire an inescapable importance. Innovation will be increasingly important also in the humanities and social sciences. Therefore it is not sufficient for us to treat research simply as a part of the training of students, or as a training regime for academics to keep themselves in condition, or as a requirement for promotion, or as a vehicle of self-dedication, although it can be all those things. Research is an activity of vital national importance, carried on variously by government, industry and universities. It is this aspect of research that is discussed in this chapter. We begin with an examination of the support of university research, for which we draw heavily on the Macdonald Report.[1]

Financial Support of Research

In 1966-67 the total income of Canadian universities and colleges for sponsored, assisted and contracted research was $80.7 million. The federal government and the provincial governments contributed $63.9 million of this. Foundations accounted for only $7 million, and business and industry, $2.7 million.[2] Municipal governments provided a negligible $81,000.

This direct income for research covers only a fraction of the universities' total commitment to research purposes. To the

---

[1] Macdonald, *et al*, *The Role of the Federal Government in Support of Research in Canadian Universities*, (Ottawa: Queen's Printer, 1968).
[2] Opportunities exist for a greater involvement of universities in research of interest to industry and efforts to stimulate such activity have been made by the Department of Industry through the establishment of Industrial Research Institutes. These are supported initially by the Department and are intended to perform university-based research for both corporate and governmental clients. The first institute was established in 1967. Three institutes are located at Ontario universities – Windsor, McMaster and Waterloo.

direct costs must be added a number of other costs associated
with salaries, libraries, computing, graduate studies, and administrative overhead. A good estimate of the total of all costs
for the year in question is $265 million. The provinces' contri-
bution to this total was about $181 million and the federal
contribution was about $67 million.

Since that time the federal government through fiscal transfer arrangements has taken over about half of the provincial
contribution, so that at the present time, for all direct and
indirect costs of university research, the federal government is
really paying about 3/5 and the provincial governments about
2/5. This is a rough calculation but there is no reason to believe that closer analysis would show a significant variation
from this 3:2 ratio of federal to provincial contributions to
university research.

Acknowledging the *de facto* situation that the provinces and
the federal government and the universities are all involved in
programs of university research, this chapter will examine the
nature of the relationships and involvement and consider what
should be the role of each of the partners.

Table F shows the basis of the estimates of $265 million for
expenditures on university research in Canada in 1966-67. To
gain some insight into the characteristics of research in universities it is necessary to take a closer look at the direct expenditures. For this purpose we turn to the year 1967-68, for which
figures are available. Direct expenditures (excluding graduate
student support) amounted to about $110 million.[3] The federal
contribution was $77 million, of which the National Research
Council provided the lion's share, $38 million, followed by the
Medical Research Council, $18.5 million. The Canada Council
provided only $3 million for assisted research. Thirty-nine de-
partments of the federal government provided grant or contract
support amounting in total to about $18 million. The largest
supporter of university research among the federal departments
was National Health and Welfare, $4.4 million, followed by the
Defence Research Board, $3.7 million, and the Atomic Energy
Commission, $2.5 million. Over $15 million of the departmen-

---

[3] The non-federal share of $33 million is an estimate based on a projection of
growth.

tal support was directed to the natural sciences and engineering; only $3 million was related to the social sciences. All of these figures indicate the low level of support for the social sciences and humanities. Actually the total of federal support of university research related to the natural sciences, engineering and medicine in 1967-68 amounted to about $71 million whereas the social sciences and humanities received only about $6 million. Of this latter total, the humanities accounted for little more than half a million dollars.

Table F. Contributions to research in Canadian universities for the year 1966-67

Item		Amount $'000.000
Provincial Contributions to Research		
1. Assisted research funds from provincial governments	12	
2. Direct research expenditures from the universities general revenue	3	
3. Research component of library acquisitions	10	
4. Research component of computing centres	2	
5. Staff salaries allocated to research	59	
6. Indirect costs of research:		
In support of assisted research expenditures	28	
In support of items 2, 3 and 4	6	
In support of staff salaries, item 5	21	
7. Support of graduate instruction	34	
8. Graduate student aid	5	181
Assisted Research Funds from Non-provincial Sources		
9. From federal sources (including graduate student aid)	67	
10. From foundations, etc	17	84
TOTAL		265

The way in which funds for sponsored, assisted and contracted research are distributed among and within universities tells much about the development of university research in Canada. In 1965-66 among 47 universities, one institution received 18 per cent of the total, five received 50 per cent, ten received 83 per cent, 21 received less than $100,000 each and 15 had no research income whatsoever. These figures illustrate the not surprising fact that vast differences in research activity exist among the universities. Heavy commitment to research is not a characteristic of all universities. Nor is it characteristic of all disciplines. Biology, chemistry, and physics each receives millions of dollars from NRC; the most that any social science has received from Canada Council is about $200,000 and only three have received this much (political science, history and sociology). Many divisions received little or no support. Examples include schools of business administration, faculties of education, faculties of law, schools of architecture, departments of music, art and theatre, and schools of nursing.

In a recent year the scale of grants awarded by the National Research Council and the Medical Research Council covered approximately two-thirds of the full-time faculty in the sciences, engineering, and medicine. In the same year the number of Canada Council grants was equivalent to about 60 per cent of full-time faculty in the social sciences and humanities. No large grants were awarded in the social sciences or humanities, the average size being $3,381 in the former and $2,161 in the latter. Most grants by the National Research Council also are small, and except for negotiated major grants, computer facilities, and Atomic Energy Control Board grants, there were no really large grants. Most fall in the $5,000 to $15,000 bracket; a very few are in the $50,000 range. Twenty-three negotiated major grants in 1968-69 were in the range of $100,000 to $500,000.

This characteristic of providing large numbers of relatively small grants applies to the federal departments as well as to the Councils. For example, Atomic Energy of Canada Limited in 1967-68 awarded 40 contracts averaging $11,300 in value; Central Mortgage and Housing Corporation awarded 16 grants averaging $32,000; Defence Research Board awarded 350 grants averaging $8,000. In fact, with the exception of the above-noted special grants administered by NRC (negotiated major, computer facilities, Atomic Energy Control Board), *grants or contracts as large as $100,000 awarded by any department of the government of Canada have been rare.* This point is emphasized because of the appearance of statements expressing concern that university research is in danger of being dominat-

ed and steered by the political or social interests of government
mission-oriented sponsors; see, for instance, the recently published report by R. Hurtubise and D. C. Rowat.[4] The facts do
not support such fears.

Direct support of research in universities by the Province of
Ontario, as shown in Table G, has grown modestly in recent
years to reach a figure of $12.6 million in 1967-68. About half
of the total support was directed to agriculture and was classi-
fied as purchased research. These funds for the most part represented commitments of the Department of Agriculture and
Food to the University of Guelph. They covered not only contract research, but also services and training of technical personnel. The existence of these sums represents an inherited relationship from the period when the Ontario Agricultural College, Ontario Veterinary College and Macdonald College were
supported by the Department of Agriculture. Now that Ontario is a heavily industrialized province, the fact that 50 per cent
of its government research grants should be in agriculture is an
inherited anomaly, but it is also an important precedent for the
funding of research in the more recent areas of social concern.

The above description of some of the main areas of financial
support for research in the universities leads to a number of
conclusions:

1. Research in the universities tends to be concentrated in a
   few universities. Small universities have limited and often
   negligible research activity.
2. Research in the universities consists mostly of small or
   modest projects undertaken by individual investigators.
3. Large-scale organized research enterprises in Canadian
   universities are few in number. To the extent that they do
   exist, they are supported almost exclusively by the National Research Council's negotiated major grants.
4. Almost no large-scale university research is conducted in
   the social sciences.
5. Direct expenditures for research in the humanities are
   very small.

---

[4] R. Hurtubise, and D. C. Rowat, *Studies on the University, Society and Government* (Ottawa: University of Ottawa Press, 1970).

Table G. Direct support by the Province of Ontario of research activities within Ontario universities in the fiscal year April 1, 1967 to March 1, 1968

Department	Grants-in-Aid[1]		Research Purchased		Scholarships & Bursaries[2]	
	Total $	Fed. Cont. $	Total $	Fed. Cont. $	Total $	Fed. Cont. $
Agriculture and Food	—	—	6,315,507	—	24,923	—
Attorney General	65,000	—			5,636	—
Correctional Services	30,000	—	40,500	7,200	4,600	—
Energy and Resources Management incl. Ontario Water Resources Commission[3]	—	—	34,925	—	12,996	—
Health[4]	752,392	538,674	127,734	—	269,185	27,738
Highways	—	—	65,000	—	5,800	—
Labour	11,400	—	12,746	—	—	—
Lands and Forests	3,000	—	73,500	—	—	—
Provincial Secretary & Citizenship	5,000	—	—	—	—	—
University Affairs	745,207	—	—	—	4,009,600	—
	1,611,999	538,674	6,669,912	7,200	4,332,740	27,738

[1] Grants-in-aid of research proposals initiated by university personnel.
[2] Scholarships and bursaries only — no loans.
[3] The University of Toronto received a grant of $130,000 on behalf of the Great Lakes Institute (not included above).
[4] The Connaught Medical Research Laboratories received directly a research grant for $27,508 (not included above). These figures exclude support of the Ontario Institute for Studies in Education which totalled $7.6 million
Data obtained from Office of Deputy Treasurer, Province of Ontario.

6. Most direct support of research in Canadian universities is provided in response to the interests of the academic community. Mission-oriented government departments have not distorted the balance of research in favour of their interests.

7. The Councils and other agencies have not provided machinery and funds to respond to requests for support in all university disciplines. Little interest in research support has been expressed by the members of some disciplines.

Science Policy for Canada

These characteristics are the result of fifty years of conventional wisdom in Canadian science policy, critically reviewed by the Senate Special Committee on Science Policy, under the chairmanship of the Honourable Maurice Lamontagne.[5] The beginnings in 1919 were presented in evidence to a special committee of the House of Commons at which time the needs of industry and the need for university training for research were recognized. Unfortunately the conclusion was accepted that Canadian industry was incapable of mounting research sufficient for its needs, that government laboratories should be established for this purpose and that universities should be supported in the training of pure researchers as a basis of meeting the manpower needs of industry and government. It is little wonder that universities have emphasized small scale basic research in the sciences over the past half century. Such research was consistent with the evolving policies of the National Research Council. Likewise it is not surprising that persons trained under such limitations have not been interested in industrial research and have not been attractive to industry. The end result well-known to most has been the development of a higher concentration of research in government laboratories than one would find in other countries. At the same time, the scientists providing manpower for the government laboratories, having been trained in universities biased in favour of basic research, have continued to display the bias, with the consequence that they have inadequately served the interests of industry.

---

[5] *A Science Policy for Canada*, Vol. 1, (Ottawa: Queen's Printer, 1970).

The policies and priorities of the last fifty years have also been responsible for the emphasis on natural sciences (and not all of them) to the exclusion of effort in the social sciences in areas crucial to public policy. This criticism of course is not unique to Canada but has been characteristic of all the developed countries of the world.

At the centre of the scientific structure in Canada has been the National Research Council. Since it provided the bulk of university support it developed close relationships with the scientists in the universities and close similarities in scientific interests. However, as observed by the Lamontagne committee, "when NRC obtained its laboratories the effectiveness of the Council as an overall science policy agency was seriously weakened. The Council could hardly perform its advisory role effectively when its president was responsible for operating laboratories in competition with not only government departments but the universities and industry too."[6]

Measured by its stated goals, Canada's science policy has been a failure or close to it. Nevertheless the results have not been all bad. The National Research Council has performed with distinction in the pure sciences and many of its scientists have had international recognition and have given Canada a place of respect in the world community of science. NRC support of universities has produced a number of strong departments of pure science and has given the country a resource of well-trained and in some cases distinguished basic scientists. The failure has been a lack of balance, a down-grading of applied science, a neglect of some fields, unconcern for national goals, and a lack of coordinated and integrated effort. Senator Lamontagne, noting the isolation from each other manifested by government, industry and the universities, has spoken of Canadian science as "the three solitudes."

It seems likely that a coordinated science policy tuned to the needs of post-industrial Canada may emerge as a result of the deliberations of the Senate Committee on Science Policy and the critiques emanating from such bodies as the Science Council of Canada and the Organization for Economic Cooperation

---

[6] *Ibid.*, p. 52.

and Development. It seems evident that the primary requirement of a successful science policy will be to separate the advisory function from the operations. As observed by the Lamontagne committee, "government research agencies are more likely to be defensive than self-critical; why should they differ from
other institutions?"[7]

The Goals of University Research

The characteristics of research in the universities largely reflect
the historical and traditional views of the role of research as a
function of the universities. Basic research has been favoured.
(The term basic research is defined for present purposes as
research undertaken as an intellectual exercise for the purpose
of broadening or deepening knowledge and having no apparent
practical objective or application.) Basic research of course – as
we have pointed out already – is not carried on exclusively in
universities. A good deal is conducted by government laboratories and some by industry although in the latter case it is usually oriented toward applied objectives. Universities, however,
carry on basic research as one of their primary responsibilities.
Though it sounds platitudinous, expansion of knowledge for its
own sake is a noble human enterprise and universities are society's primary custodian of this activity.

Acknowledging this fact does not provide answers to the
difficult questions about the levels of support universities
should receive for basic research or the relationships between
research and teaching activities within the universities and colleges. In the last analysis the answer to the former question
represents a decision about public policy. The problems are
both political and technical. What level of support should basic
research receive from the public purse, given the wide range of
other high priority objectives of Canadian society? How shall
the demand for research support be evaluated, bearing in mind
numbers and quality of applicants, quality and significance of
proposals, and dollar requirements for adequate performance?

Without attempting to provide the complete answers we

---

[7] *Ibid.*, p. 279.

make the following general observations. In the society of the future, heavily dependent on science and technology, continuing stable support of basic research is needed to provide an expanding reservoir of knowledge on which to draw for the innovations which will contribute solutions to practical problems. We quoted Joseph Ben-David at length in the last chapter on the relationship between fundamental discoveries and practical interests. As we said, it would be an impoverishment of Canada to neglect the support of basic research in a future that will be so irretrievably dependent on complex knowledge. This knowledge, we reiterate, will be drawn from research in the humanities and social sciences as well as the sciences.

Not all academics are qualified to conduct basic research and the mere holding of a university appointment does not confer a right to support for research activities. We have suggested earlier, in fact, that an obligation to research created by the academic sub-culture may force some professors into an activity which they find irksome and to which they may not be suited. They would rather teach. Those wishing to conduct research must have their qualifications and their proposals subjected to rigorous adjudication by their peers. There is good reason to question the adequacy of the process in review conducted by many of the granting agencies.

Applied research, although sometimes looked upon by academics as being somehow inferior, requires in fact the same high level of competence and training as basic research if it is to be performed well. Universities in Canada, happily, are giving more recognition to applied research than in earlier years, especially in the professional faculties. This is demonstrated by the strengthening of clinical investigation in medicine, the growing commitment of engineering schools to research, the interest of law faculties in research related to law reform, increasing attention to urban problems, etc. Such developments should be welcomed and encouraged, not at the expense of proper attention to and support of basic research, but as a way in which universities can more productively fulfil their role as catalysts and critics of society, and as providers of information needed for making public policy.

Applied research can be performed by individuals or small groups in ways which parallel the usual performance of basic research. But it can also be undertaken as large-scale organized research involving major commitments of manpower and resources. This type of mission-oriented research if supported by government represents an approach chosen to achieve some goal considered by government to be desirable; in short it represents an approach to a social objective. University members are divided on the advisability of the universities becoming engaged in such large-scale research missions as noted in the Macdonald Report.[8] We draw on that Report in what appears below.

The fear of some is that if Canadian universities engage in large-scale contract research in the public interest they will be distracted from basic research and more particularly from teaching. This fear is founded on experiences in the United States where some universities have become so heavily engaged in contract research for the Federal Government that their whole character has been distorted. It has been suggested that much of the student feeling of neglect and many of charges of irrelevancy of teaching is attributable to preoccupation of faculty with these major research undertakings.

Those who see a role for the university in public research missions argue that Canada cannot afford to establish large government research installations divorced from graduate training, that much of the research required by government (and perhaps industry) would be suitable for the training of graduate students, and that the universities have a large resource of research manpower which could be used more effectively in the Canadian interest than is now the case. We would argue for the involvement of some universities in large-scale contract research, within carefully defined limits. To begin with, it is self-evident that the university must have society's support. In return, society must have access to the university's resources. There is no escape from that conclusion in the modern world. The urgency of the issues facing society, the dispassionate, non-political objectivity of the universities, the wealth of human resources within the university, and the fact that in many instances no other institution has the capacity to meet the challenge, all are compelling reasons why the university

---

[8]Macdonald, *et al.*, *op. cit.*

117

must be prepared to give service in appropriate circumstances.

Such appropriate circumstances would exist where a government-sponsored mission was consistent with the university's long-term goals, including in particular its graduate teaching, and did not interfere with other commitments or overstrain the total organization.

Contract research arrangements of this kind would help to develop additional trained manpower and would strengthen interchange between the university and society, since the university would be performing an important public service. But difficulties exist, of two types. The first is an organizational one: policies with respect to tenure and freedom to pursue one's own line of investigation have not in the past lent themselves readily to organized large-scale research missions. Some of these policies, as we have indicated, are overdue for change; and besides, it is greatly to the interest of the universities to overcome this difficulty one way or another. "Big science" is becoming more important in modern research, not only in the natural sciences and engineering but also in the social sciences and the health sciences. Without forsaking "little science", universities should recognize an obligation to demonstrate and teach the methods of "big science" because many of their graduates will be called upon to work in that area.

The second difficulty with contract research arrangements is that government might be led to look upon the university as a pool of talent automatically on call. They would need to be reminded constantly that teaching and research are the primary responsibilities of the university; service to society, however important, must come after the responsibilities to students. The talent existing within universities is available in the first instance for the internal purposes of the university, and only if proposals are consistent with the university's primary responsibilities should they be undertaken by the university. Government departments should look upon the possibility of making use of the university as a privilege, not a right. In the long run, society will be best served by adherence to this view of the role of the universities.

The final role of research in universities relates to the function of universities as teaching institutions. Much has been written, pro and con, about the effect of research activity on the quality of teaching. We do not propose to review the arguments but simply state that university teaching aimed at fulfilling its highest aspiration, that of generating a spirit of critical enquiry, cannot be divorced from research. This is probably more true of the specialist undergraduate instruction than of the generalist which we differentiated earlier. The proposition is certainly true of graduate teaching. Whatever the price in divided interests, in a feeling by students that the interests of teachers are in the subject, not the student, in ambiguous promotion policies, in charges of irrelevancy, the price must be paid – if not in all institutions, at least in those leading ones which should emerge with the increasing differentiation of the Ontario system. Without research as an integral part of the academic system, the student and society cannot gain the qualities of criticism and renewal which the university must create if it is to be a distinctive and crucial institution.

A second aspect of the relationship of research to the teaching function of the university is the fact that the university is responsible for training the high-level manpower to conduct research. This is not a mere self-serving function though it is part of the process of qualifying persons to be academics. Research manpower is needed outside the universities by government, business and industry and there is every reason to believe this need will grow more or less steadily for a long time despite present short-term economic conditions. The training of research manpower is a central function of graduate education and obviously it can only be performed in an environment where research is being conducted.

As we have noted, the characteristics of post-industrial society will differ greatly from those of the period of industrial society now terminating. Some features of future society will bear heavily on the universities' responsibilities for research. Decisions about the introduction of technical innovations will be based on more sophisticated evaluation of ecological consequences and on more skilful planning and management. The resources for planning, forecasting, and systems analysis will reside largely with governments, universities and research organizations. Effective and successful performance of these functions will depend on the degree to which they are based on values widely held in society. This chain of inter-locking characteristics means that universities will need to become more responsive to society's aspirations and more committed to ser-

119

vice. This change need not result in a diminution of emphasis on teaching and research for its own sake, but rather in an added dimension to the work of universities.

We have noted that many students are deeply concerned with the university's commitment to the service of society. In some instances, however, this legitimate concern is being twisted into a demand that universities operate as political forces seeking to impose their particular notions of utopia on a reluctant society.

A better alternative exists. Universities need to develop organizational skills to bring their specialized resources to bear on the complex problems of society. Such problems are numerous and will represent a major preoccupation of post-industrial society. Currently they include such diverse issues as environmental pollution, delivery systems for health care, improving upward mobility for disadvantaged groups, crime and rehabilitation, energy policies, transportation systems, etc. Current efforts by universities in all these areas tend to be fragmented and partial. Obviously, comprehensive approaches cannot be developed by individual investigators; but the composite resources of universities, if organized to do so, could contribute to providing answers to many of these great problems. The task in most cases will need to engage the capacities of a wide variety of specialists drawn from the sciences, social sciences and the professions. The solutions generated by universities in this way will surely increase the relevance of universities; at the same time they will provide society with sound and practical means of dealing with its problems. Moreover, the universities can thus serve society better without destroying themselves by becoming political instruments.

Universities in the future therefore will develop new forms of interdisciplinary organizations which may be institutes, centres, task forces, or consortia designed to propose solutions to major complex problems of society. (We have suggested in Chapter Seven that these groupings will be more transient than they are now, more capable of being rapidly assembled and dismantled in relation to changing needs.) Society, of course, will be left with the hard political choices involved in accepting or rejecting proposed solutions regardless of how skilfully the universities may assess the benefits and costs among the alternatives. At the same time, universities will continue their traditional research roles in conducting basic research, enhancing teaching, and training researchers.

The Federal Role in the Support of Research

The area of research has been of particular concern to the federal government, as was manifested as early as 1917 when the National Research Council began to make grants-in-aid of research and to award scholarships and fellowships. The federal concern is strikingly evident in the recent remarkable growth of support for university research, which rose (in the sciences) from $12 million in 1959-60 to $101 million in 1968-69. It is also evident in the terms of the Canada Council Act, 1957, designed to foster and promote the study and enjoyment of and production of work in the arts, humanities and social sciences.

There has also, of course, been a more general concern of the federal government for the welfare of the universities, as expressed in the series of arrangements for direct grants and (since 1967) fiscal transfers. In proposing the current arrangements the then Prime Minister, Mr. Pearson, stated that "education is obviously a matter of profound importance to the economic and social structure of the country as a whole. This is particularly true of higher education."

These historical developments fully justify the statement that the federal government has maintained an interest in strong universities and that that interest has been expressed in part through its direct support of university research.

A second involvement of the federal government is the procurement of research from the universities. As a large number of government departments require research in relation to their departmental responsibilities, these departments carry on the majority of their research intramurally. Although the total allocated to universities is not large, the amount is growing and it involves a large number of departments. As universities begin to develop competence for large-scale organized research, the interests of governments in procuring research from them is likely to increase; it seems likely that in the future this aspect of university-government relationships may become very important.

The Division of Costs

The present handling of costs creates difficulties for both governments and universities. The federal government has found it difficult to tolerate the open-ended feature of the fiscal transfer arrangements. The provinces have been pressed by the universi-

121

ties to meet the indirect costs of research that is growing at a rate over which provincial governments have little or no control. And the universities – especially the older ones with large programs of research – have been hard-pressed to cover the indirect costs of research, and are in fact making ends meet at the expense of some of their teaching/learning activities. It can hardly be otherwise in provinces where provincial grants are tied to enrolment and do not reflect the volume of research activity. The problem is further aggravated by the policies of the research councils and some government departments of providing only grants-in-aid of direct research costs, rather than covering all the costs of the research which they support.

We believe that the basis of a solution of these dilemmas is for the federal government and the provinces to agree, not to *share* costs, but to *divide* them, with each of the parties accepting full responsibility for certain categories of costs. In this way the distortions and pressures created by open-ended agreements and by unilateral decisions can be greatly diminished, if not eliminated.

If the principle of divided costs rather than shared costs is adopted, the problem becomes one of agreeing upon the division of the categories of costs for which each party would accept responsibility. This should be a matter for intensive joint discussion, perhaps for a federal-provincial conference. So far as research is concerned, the aim must be to find a division of responsibilities that enables all the partners in the activity to realize their legitimate aims.

CHAPTER 10

THE
FEDERAL
ROLE

We start from the premise that post-secondary education must be the concern of both levels of government in this country – provincial *and* federal.

It would be tidier, of course, and less of a strain on federal-provincial cooperation, if post-secondary education were the concern of only one level of government. It would be particularly tidy if this level were the federal one for then everything to do with the subject-matter would fall under a single umbrella. And certainly this would be preferable to the recent extraordinary proposal that everything should fall under ten disparate provincial umbrellas with no federal involvement at all.[1] But neither a complete centralization nor a complete decentralization really answers the needs of the situation. Both levels of government must be concerned.

René Hurtubise and Donald C. Rowat, "The University, Society and Government," *Report of the Commission on the Relations between Universities and Governments* (Ottawa: University of Ottawa Press, 1970).

123

The case for provincial concern is obvious. Basic to all else is Section 93 of the British North America Act which provides that "In and for each Province the Legislature may exclusively make Laws in relation to Education. . . ." The qualifying phrase here, of course, is "In and for each Province" and we shall have more to say about this when discussing constitutional supports for the federal government's role. Even with this qualification, however, ample scope remains for provincial governments to legislate with respect to education, including post-secondary education, if they so wish.

Until after the second World War the provinces did not, in fact, give a high priority to university and college education. They did charter new institutions from time to time and most of them gave varying, and fluctuating, degrees of financial assistance, but the universities were expected to find other benefactors as well. As J. A. Corry, former Principal of Queen's, has pointed out, even the provincially supported institutions "were not considered to be the exclusive responsibility of the provinces."[2] Furthermore, the universities themselves, in their appeals to business, industry and private benefactors, did so on the grounds that "they were private institutions catering to a national (and in some respects international) constituency."

With the enormous increase in student enrolments in the post World War II period, however, the universities simply could not, through their own efforts, or with the sporadic assistance of provincial (and federal) governments, meet their growing costs of operation, costs that rose from $76 million in 1954-55 to $579 million in 1966-67. By the late 1950's, all universities and most provincial governments had recognized the need for massive governmental assistance.

Financial help on such a large scale involved the provinces even more deeply. With so much money flowing into the universities, provincial governments became increasingly concerned about educational policy and planning at the post-secondary level – how many new universities there should be, what other kinds of post-secondary institutions, if any, what

---

[2] J. A. Corry, *Farewell the Ivory Tower* (Montreal: McGill-Queen's University Press, 1970), pp. 42-43.

124

new professional schools and where, how many teachers, and so on. When a government is putting a good deal of its taxpayers' money into something, it must take some interest in how the money is being spent. This is true even in such a sensitive area as higher education.

For other reasons, too, apart from the need for public accountability, provincial governments have had, and continue to have, a vital interest in policy. They may, for example, wish to see some part of the post-secondary system take account of their peculiar regional needs – forestry, agriculture, mining, Indian affairs, and so on. More broadly, there will undoubtedly be a concern, on the part of every province, to see that the labour force needs of its own economy are met by its university and college system. Indeed, it is partly because of this concern that so many provinces in recent years have developed new post-secondary institutions – CAATs in Ontario, CEGEPs in Quebec, community colleges in British Columbia.

Nor can a province be indifferent to the kind of citizen it is producing and the role being played by its institutions of higher learning in this process. Above all, it will surely want to ensure, through its student aid programs, a greater democratization of educational opportunity at the post-secondary level throughout the province. This it will want to do not only for manpower reasons but on grounds of equity as well.

As we have said, there is no need to elaborate the provinces' need to be involved in post-secondary educational policy and planning nowadays, whatever may have been their attitudes earlier in our history. Let us therefore turn to the case for a federal involvement.

The case for a federal involvement is not quite as obvious as the provincial one since it is something we tend not to talk about in this country. This is surprising, since there has been a federal concern in aspects of higher education for a very long time, at least since 1876, when the federal government established a Royal Military College in Kingston to support its defence responsibilities.

A substantial part of the federal involvement, as noted in chapter nine, has been in the area of research. The federal government has also had a long-standing interest in providing loans to students. It began with educational loans to veterans after the first World War and after the second World War it

125

went even further and provided outright educational grants to
all qualified veterans. For students in financial need a loan
fund was started in 1939, a shared-cost program with the provinces, called the Dominion-Provincial Student Aid Program
The most ambitious loan scheme, however, was the one started
in 1964, the Canada Student Loans Plan, under which we are
operating today.

A third important area of federal concern has been in providing grants to the universities themselves. That the federal
government would be a quite legitimate body to turn to for
such financial assistance was revealed as early as 1885 at the
annual meeting of the Royal Society of Canada, when the Society stated that:

> "... No one of our colleges has anything like a pro-
> per equipment ... grants might be given either by
> *Central* or Local Governments to all our universi-
> ties ..."[3] (Italics added).

Again, in the Rowell-Sirois Report of 1940 it was argued that
there might be "a relatively small Dominion annual grant divided among the provinces in rough proportion to their population"[4] for the benefit of their universities. And, of course, the
Massey Report of 1951 made a very strong case for federal
grants to universities, arguing that "... if financial stringency
prevents these great institutions from being, as they have said,
'nurseries of a truly Canadian civilization and culture', we are
convinced that this is a matter of national concern."[5]

At the time of the Massey Report the provinces were certainly not showing any inclination to increase their support. The
grants they were then making to the universities were only
three times what they had been in 1920, whereas total provincial expenditures had increased six and a half times. In any
event, the federal government took action in 1951 and began

---

[3] *Proceedings and Transactions of the Royal Society of Canada*, First Series,
Volume III (1885), p. 4.
[4] *Report of the Royal Commission on Dominion-Provincial Relations* (Ottawa:
Queen's Printer, 1940), Book II, p. 52
[5] *Report of the Royal Commission on National Development in the Arts, Letters
and Sciences* (Ottawa: Queen's Printer, 1951), p. 143.

making direct grants to the universities. It continued this program until 1967. Capital grants were also provided, through the
Canada Council, for a number of years.

Finally, in 1967, with the termination of the direct grants
program, the federal government began making fiscal transfers
to the provinces, making available to them fifty per cent of the
operating costs incurred by their post-secondary educational
institutions. This program continues today.

Ottawa, then, has created colleges such as RMC, supported
research, given scholarships and grants to students and made
direct grants to universities, as well as the fiscal transfers to the
provinces. There is no shortage of precedents for a continuing
federal involvement in the years ahead.[6]

Quite apart from the precedents, however, there are several
strong grounds for a federal presence in higher education today, grounds that may assume an even larger significance in the
future. For example, we have in this country not only ten provincial economies but one integrated national economy which
only the federal government can (or will) look at *in toto*. Developing national economic policies must, therefore, be one of the
federal government's primary concerns. What our national economic policies will be, however, is determined, in part at least,
by the state of our higher learning. And so, what goes into and
comes out of our universities must be of more than passing
interest to the federal government.

This is particularly obvious in the case of high-level manpower skills since these are central to our national economic
development. There has been some evidence of federal concern
in the development of these skills (through its scholarship and
research programs, for example), but there has also been a very
heavy reliance on the importation of skills. Indeed:

> For the top two classes, that is, the occupations
> having the highest scale values, the proportion of
> the native-born labour force, compared to the post-

---

[6]The most distressing aspect of the Rowat-Hurtubise Report (cf. footnote 1) is
its eagerness to abandon all the precedents for a federal role in higher education. Surely no policies for the future can ever be built on a total rejection of
the past.

war immigrant labour force in them is strikingly
different. In Ontario the proportion of the native-
born labour force in these two classes was 9.9 per
cent, but that of post-war UK immigrants was 17.8
per cent, and of post-war US immigrants 28.2 per
cent. In the western provinces the proportions were
8.7 per cent of the native-born labour force, 14.4 per
cent of the UK, and 31.8 per cent of the US. In
Quebec the Canadian-born proportion was 7.35, the
UK 29.6 and the US-born 35.3. These proportions
indicate how much richer in trained capacity than
the native-born labour force were the post-war immigrants who came from the United Kingdom and
the United States.[7]

It would be inconceivable if the federal government's contem
porary concern with manpower training and retraining at th
lowest levels of skills were to preclude a concern with the high
est, most mobile skills simply because these are the ones tha
are produced by our institutions of higher learning.

Also in the field of national economic policy is the federa
concern, shared by all political parties, with regional in
equalities. A nation can hardly be held together if parts of it
are seriously disadvantaged economically. But to get at the
problem of regional economic inequalities one must tackle th
problem of education since the development of education i
fundamental to the greater equalization of regional economi
opportunities. Nor are general equalization formulae sufficient
There have to be specialized, specially directed federal policies
to strengthen education in disadvantaged areas.

There is also a need for federal concern in the fulfillment of
our obligations to the developing world, in the providing, for
example, of certain skills and educational opportunities.

Finally, the case for a federal involvement in higher education relates to our very identity as a nation:

[7]Taken from John Porter's article "Post-Nationalism, Post-Industrialism and
Post-Secondary Education", to be published in a forthcoming issue of the
Canadian Public Administration, Spring, 1971.

> . . . if there is indeed a nation to be spoken for and
> protected, then the federal government must speak
> for the nation, take steps to ensure its survival and
> nourish its growth. If the nation is also a living
> community, it cannot be shut out of all influence in
> the direction of education. At times, it may be that
> mere adding up of the educational effort of ten
> provinces will give a sum that covers federal concern
> in education. At other times, it will not, and then
> Parliament and the Government of Canada must
> have the power to give special emphasis and some
> direction to selected aspects of education.[8]

The fact that we are a nation embracing two official languages
makes a strong federal role in higher education even more
urgent. The 'truly Canadian civilization and culture' for which
our universities are the nurseries must be a French-Canadian
civilization and culture as well as an English-speaking one.

Given the arguments for a federal concern we must now ask
– what form or forms should the federal role take? There are
probably as many different answers to this question as there
are people asking it. And no single answer may be the right
one, or permanently right.

Two points are essential. One is that the federal role should
not consist simply of the government's turning large amounts
of money over to the provinces, as in the present fiscal transfer
arrangements. Such a practice is an abrogation of the whole
principle of public accountability. It is doubtful, indeed, if the
public even knows that fifty percent of post-secondary operating expenditures are being provided by the federal government
today. Furthermore, it is a denial of any genuine policy role,
beyond the federal government's being "pro-education" in
making so much money available to the provinces. And a
strong policy role, as we have argued, is essential. Finally, it
creates uncertainty, both for the federal government, which
cannot know how much money will be involved in any given
year, and for the provinces, who cannot be sure that the program will even continue for another five-year period.

---

[8]Corry, *op. cit.*, pp. 40-41.

It is essential, therefore, that whatever the nature of the federal government's continuing involvement in higher education both the federal government and the provinces should have fairly clear bailiwicks to operate in, each level of government having its own responsibilities, each level financing its responsibilities. In other words, the basic principle we should operate on is one of divided costs and divided powers, rather than the present pattern of shared costs and indeterminate federal powers.

The second point to bear in mind is that our proposals are not designed to make the federal government's role less costly in the future than it is today. The contrary may well be the case. Meanwhile, as changes in the federal role are being worked out over the next ten to fifteen years, we would expect that the federal government's financial contribution would be no less, in any aspect of post-secondary education, than it is at present and that, in particular, the fiscal transfer arrangements would be continued during the re-shaping period.

Turning to the ways in which a federal involvement can be more fully and sharply realized in the future, an obvious candidate is the field of research. The federal presence in research could well be extended, both through increasing direct federal support of university research and through the greater procurement, by government departments, of research from the universities.

So far as direct federal support of university research is concerned, much more is possible. Indeed, we recommend that the federal government, through its research councils, accept the responsibility for maintaining a rational program of university research which is balanced and covers the needs of all disciplines. Such federal support should not be restricted in subject matter. As former Prime Minister L. B. Pearson once pointed out:

> . . . research, as the means by which we expand the frontier of knowledge, is today one of the most important factors in the economic and social growth of any modern political society. The restriction of federal aid to research to subject matters that are within federal legislative jurisdiction would frustrate the purposes of the scientific spirit.

If this country is to have an active and vigorous research program which will redound to the advantage of all its citizens and add effectively to our fund of knowledge, governments at any level must feel free to sponsor and support research of any kind without being limited by conceivable legal classifications of its results or its end use. Failure by the federal government to play its full share in such a national task could only mean that Canada's ability to take part in the undertakings of today which are shaping the world of tomorrow would be seriously impaired.[9]

It is vitally important, however, that the federal government bear the full cost of the research it chooses to support. At the present time the provinces make major contributions to it through funding of academic salaries, library costs, computing costs, support of graduate students and coverage of the indirect costs of research sponsored by the federal government. We recommend that the federal government accept responsibility for some, at least, of these costs, as follows:

1. The full direct costs of that research which it supports. At present the policy of the research councils and some departments is to provide grants in aid of direct costs rather than to cover all the direct costs of the research they support. This tends to force universities with large research programs to divert funds to the support of research which should be devoted to other purposes. In an earlier era, when universities were less dependent on governments and when research was less expensive and its importance less clearly recognized, the philanthropic posture may have been reasonable. Today it is unrealistic and unwise. In keeping with the view that research is a partnership, performed by the university and paid for by government, nothing short of a careful assessment of the costs, and award of grants sufficient to cover them, represents sound policy.

---

[9]Statement by the Prime Minister for the Federal-Provincial Meeting, October 24, 1966, pp. 26-27.

2. The indirect costs of research which it supports. These should be paid for essentially similar reasons as those described above. Failure to meet these costs has meant that federal grants have seriously distorted the universities' budgetary processes. It is not an answer that the federal government pays indirect costs through fiscal transfers. These moneys are paid to the provinces after the universities have incurred the costs. Moreover, they will cover only fifty per cent of the indirect costs for which the universities have paid. We recommend that the indirect cost allowance payable by federal agencies over and above direct research support be thirty-five per cent of the direct research support given to each university.

3. The cost of graduate student support. There is a federal interest here, deriving from the need to provide research manpower. Also, as noted earlier, high level manpower is extremely mobile and most provinces retain less than half of the Ph. D.'s they train, (Ontario is the one exception). These interests can be served by a program of competitive national scholarships operated through the research councils and offering prestigious recognition to the most promising students.

4. The cost of university buildings or parts of buildings which can be identified clearly as research facilities. Capital facilities for research represent an important part of the requirement of a viable policy of research support. The federal government should, therefore, as part of its responsibility for supporting university research, accept the necessity of providing the facilities in which it is to be conducted. If a program of federal support for research buildings is introduced, conditions should be placed on applicant institutions so that they identify the amount and source of funds for parts of buildings which would not be covered by a research facilities grant.[10]

---

[10] Since Ontario is moving toward the introduction of a formula for determining capital entitlement, the proposal for federal payment for research buildings would have important implications, and the formula would need to be adjusted to exclude research buildings for which the federal government was providing the capital.

would also of course continue its relationships with universities
in the province. The difference would be that the federal government would be concerned with the universities only with
respect to their graduate and higher degree professional work
and, also, with the bulk of their research work since this is
chiefly performed at these levels. It would also have a direct
relationship with the students concerned.

There are many advantages to such a scheme. For one thing,
it establishes more sharply than the other alternatives the principle of divided responsibility. And, as we have already argued,
it is better for the federal government to have a reasonably
clear responsibility than one that is likely to overlap or unduly
interfere with provincial responsibilities. So, too, the costs
would be divided rather than shared and this would make it
possible to focus responsibility. The public would know who
was paying for what. The provincial governments, too, would
surely prefer a fairly clear-cut division of responsibilities and
costs than the present scheme of not knowing when the rug
might be pulled out from under them.

Furthermore, with the federal government having its role
delineated in this way it would be able to plan, develop and
coordinate the highly skilled manpower and research requirements of the nation, relating both, to some extent, to its overall
social and economic policies, including science policies. It
would be able to coordinate, in a way that is not now possible,
all the disparate provincial programs at the post-graduate and
post-first degree professional levels and develop the more rational use of resources where it is simply not feasible for every
province to try to do everything. In short, on both economic
and educational grounds such a role for the federal government
would be desirable.

As for constitutional supports, it will be recalled that the BNA
Act gives the provinces power to legislate with respect to education "in and for each province." The implication is that when
education is not simply in and for each province but for the
whole nation (and, indeed, for the international community) it
becomes a legitimate concern, under the residual clause of the
BNA Act, of the federal government. Post-graduate and post-
first degree professional education, and research, are today and
will be even more over the next decade or two "in and for the
nation" and the world.

The proposal does, of course, present difficulties. There would be a number of administrative hurdles to leap in working out the detailed division of such important common costs as academic salaries in many instances, library facilities, laboratories, buildings, and so on. Administrative hurdles are, however, not insurmountable. More serious, the proposal might not be politically acceptable to the provinces, even in time. Quebec would perhaps find it alarming, and might wish to opt out, which would be most unfortunate. On the other hand, there are a number of people in *all* the provinces, particularly in the scientific and some of the professional communities, who see the great need for a clear defined federal presence at the highest levels of our educational ladder. Their voices may be heard more frequently and more strongly – in Quebec, too – over the next few years.

It should perhaps be made clear at this point that we do not envisage, either in connection with this proposal or the ones before, that a federal *department* of government would itself engage massively in direct relationships with universities or students. There would, of course, be a federal department, but the detailed relationships would be conducted by an intervening body which would develop the necessary grant structures, formulas, appraisal systems, and so on, whether the federal government's role was with institutions or with students or both.

There might well be provincial governmental as well as academic representation on this intervening body and for certain planning purposes the federal government might work through regional agencies that are made up of the academic and government representatives in the region. Only very broad matters of policy and, of course, the parameters of the budget, would rest with the federal government as such.

But with respect to overall policy and budget, a department is essential, with its own minister and adequate staff. Indeed, whatever the role of the federal government with respect to post-secondary education, there should be a minister and department to make the federal presence effective, effective not only with other ministers and departments in Ottawa, but with all provincial departments of education as well.

None of this, of course, will come overnight. It will take a great deal of initiative, not only on the part of the federal government but of the provinces as well. A province like Ontario, big enough and strong enough to "go it alone" in all aspects of education, might be tempted to try. This would be disastrous, not only for Ontario and many other provinces, but for the nation as a whole.

Nor can changes be made over the next decade or two without a great deal of discussion between the two levels of government. (Perhaps the next constitutional conference would be a good place to start). It is particularly incumbent upon the federal government to take no new steps without discussing them fully with the provinces. Total agreement is not necessary so long as the federal government is exercising its responsibilities within the constitution. Too often in the past the federal government engaged in educational programs – the percapita grants, student loans, fiscal transfers, etc. – without informing the provinces. The result has been irritation, duplication and, frequently, withdrawal.

It is vital that the federal government *should* exercise its constitutional responsibilities in the field of higher education. Undoubtedly a clearer role for the federal government will emerge in stages over the next decade or two. Any combination of our proposals, or the last proposal alone, could be phased in gradually. The important thing is that we recognize now that all provinces need a voice to speak for the nation as a whole. We will need it even more urgently in the decades ahead and we will need it, above all, in the field of education. By ensuring that the federal government has certain clear-cut responsibilities in the field, in areas such as we have outlined, and by ensuring that its role is effectively integrated both in Ottawa and with the provincial governments, a new day of creative federalism in the field of higher education can dawn.

CHAPTER 11

THE
ALLOCATION
OF
COSTS

One of the most appealing prospects about the creative federalism envisaged in the last chapter is that it will be possible to
look at the educational requirements of the whole of Canadian
society as well as at particular local, regional and provincial
needs. Post-industrialism will bring the most advanced societies of the world into increasingly extensive linkages with one
another, and will produce new needs for trans-national cooperation. Post-industrial societies will also have obligations to pre-
industrial, newly-developing parts of the world. There will be
continued if not increasing need for the kind of economic and
administrative and academic assistance that has been provided
by English-speaking Canadian university personnel in the West
Indies, Sierra Leone, Tanzania, etc., and by French-speaking
Canadians in francophone countries. And until such time as
those countries have local universities adequate to their needs,
the training of their graduate students who come to Canadian
universities will be an important part of Canada's external responsibilities. All this is in addition to the internal responsibility to foster the national economy, develop a national science

138

policy, and encourage a Canadian cultural identity, which was stressed in the previous chapter.

In that chapter, we recommended that federal government involvement in post-secondary education be on a divided cost basis rather than a shared cost basis, and we suggested various alternatives that did no violence to the constitution. In turning now to discuss costs of the Ontario system we do not assume that any one particular alternative will be adopted. We think it likely that no one proposal will meet with federal and provincial favour and that some "mix" will probably result. We do, however, take it for granted that in the long run the federal government will be contributing *no less* than it does now through the fiscal transfer arrangements. Accordingly when we speak of percentages of the provincial budget going for the support of education in the future we are assuming, then as now, a massive amount of federal assistance.

The year 1970 saw a great deal of public concern being expressed about the costs of post-secondary education, which during the late sixties rose very rapidly. There have been a number of estimates of these costs and their further projections over the next several years. Dr. Douglas Wright, Chairman of the Ontario Committee on University Affairs, in observing that costs rose during this period at the rate of nearly 25 per cent per annum, suggests that "total costs can be expected to continue to increase at a compounding rate of 15 per cent or more per annum through at least to the mid-70's, if we continue our presently established policies and beliefs."[1] Similarly, Arthur J. R. Smith, Chairman of the Economic Council of Canada, stated that "Government expenditures on university education for operating purposes increased during the 1960's at about 22 per cent per year, about three times as fast as the gross national product." He notes also that "The Economic Council, in its *Sixth Annual Review*, estimated that educational expenditures would rise at a rate of about 8½ per cent per year in constant

---

[1] Douglas T. Wright, "The Financing of Post-Secondary Education: Basic Issues and Distribution of Costs," paper for the National Seminar on the Costs of Post-Secondary Education, Institute of Public Administration of Canada, June 1970, p.6.

dollars over the period 1967 to 1975, and perhaps in the range of 12 to 14 per cent per year in current dollars – that is, about twice as fast as spending on all other types of goods and services taken together. These are obviously very high rates of increase, although they reflect substantially reduced rates of increase over those previously occurring. ... actual spending since 1967 has in fact been running ahead faster than the average annual rates estimated by the Council for the 1967-75 period." But he continues with the note that "...1970-75 rates of growth should perhaps be well below those of the past few years."[2]

The Economic Council of Canada, which in its earlier reports had placed great emphasis on the importance of education to economic growth and productivity, in its September 1970 *Seventh Annual Review* joined other economists who were growing fearful of the escalated costs. It pointed out that the current level of government expenditures on higher education exceeded $2 billion. Its projection of continuing increases to 1975 was 15 per cent per annum in constant dollars, compared to 5 per cent at the elementary and secondary levels.[3] An important feature of these costs besides their obvious escalation has been the shift in the proportion of the total which has been transferred from individual students to governments. Dr. Slater estimated that for Ontario in 1969-70 roughly 77 per cent of costs were borne by public treasuries. This may be compared to 63 per cent in 1961-62 and about 80 per cent in 1970-71.[4] It is noteworthy that this view coincides closely with the estimate in the Bladen Report which estimated that 70 per cent of operating costs and 80 per cent of capital costs would have to be borne by government.[5]

In the perspective which we are striving to maintain in this

[2] Arthur J. R. Smith, "Some Economic Aspects of Education," notes for lecture at the Ontario Institute for Studies in Education, Toronto, January 1971, pp. 17-18.
[3] *Patterns of Growth*, Economic Council of Canada, Seventh Annual Review (Ottawa: Queen's Printer, 1970), p. 59.
[4] David W. Slater, "Economics of Universities and Colleges" (paper for the Canadian Economic Association, Winnipeg, June 1970), p. 5.
[5] *Financing Higher Education in Canada* (Association of Universities and Colleges of Canada, 1965), p. 36.

brief, that of the post-industrial society into which we are rapidly moving, increasing enrolments and an increasing shift of the costs from private to public resources should be viewed as social progress through the provision of more accessible post-secondary education, particularly since in Ontario as well as in other parts of Canada the system of higher education has been slow to develop. Long perspectives are, however, uncharacteristic of debate over pressing social priorities. Immediate and resentful horror at increasing costs was the dominant theme of public comment during most of 1970. Consequently, we have seen the concoction of schemes designed to change our "presently established policies and beliefs" by either limiting entry to university or shifting the burden of costs in some measure back on the individual. One argument for such a reversal has been, as the Economic Council of Canada put it, that "the rising demands and expectations for higher education are coming into sharper confrontation with alternative claims upon scarce resources."[6]

With regard to limitations on entry to university, Smith observes:

> ... a few university officials have been suggesting in recent months that the best way to contain rising governmental expenditures on education would be to move towards more restrictive procedures affecting admissions into university.

This solution, he points out, is unsatisfactory:

> University education, largely publicly financed, is already thought to discriminate in favour of the upper and middle income groups, and restricting enrolment would provoke further charges of "elitism" ... [and would be] ... an unacceptable approach.[7]

In introducing one scheme to shift costs more to private resources Professor A. R. Dobell writes:

> The fundamental problem is that the claim upon the

Patterns of Growth, p. 56.
Smith, op. cit., pp 22-23.

resources of the community for purposes of post-secondary education is already large, and is growing explosively. The real costs of meeting this claim are the other goals the community must forego in order to free the resources required to mount the educational programs demanded. There is no free education, under any circumstances; there is only the question who pays. Education may be made free to the student while he is a student, but in the rest of the community someone's consumption of medical services, or transportation, or food, or environmental improvements, or something must be reduced to free the resources required for education.[8]

It is perfectly true that education – at all levels, not solely post-secondary – imposes costs and thereby preempts part of society's resources. But this is true of all goods and services. Some observers seem to have taken alarm that the costs of education have increased at a faster rate than the productivity of the economy as a whole. This also is true of many other goods and services. It appears to us, largely because of the size of budgets and their increases, that post-secondary education is the preferred scapegoat and whipping-boy.

We should remind ourselves that when the Economic Council began its first significant research on the economic aspects of education before the mid-1960's it stated:

... the overall rates of return to the economy for investment in education were perhaps in the range of 10-15 per cent per year – on the whole, higher than the returns in investment in physical investment ... the pay-off from such investment should be explicitly recognized as being long-term in nature – in other words, that greatly increased educational efforts in the 1960's would probably produce some of their significant results only in the 1980's and

---

[8]G. A. Cook and D. A. Stager, *Student Financial Assistance Programs* (Foreword by A. R. Dobell) Toronto: Institute for the Quantitative Analysis of Social and Economic Policy, University of Toronto, 1969.

1990's, just as the low contribution of education to growth in the 1950's reflected inadequate educational efforts in the 1920's and 1930's (leading, for example, to large numbers of people in the labour force in the 1950's with eight years or less of formal schooling) . . .[9]

Similarly, Slater says:

The process of slowing down the commitments of resources to universities is now under way, at a time when the most severe pressures of the decade are developing. Too little and too late university development in Canada in the later 1950's and the early 1960's seems likely to be followed by cutbacks that are too big and too soon in the early 1970's.[10]

We would be remiss if we ignored a third alternative to limiting entry or shifting cost burden; that of improving "productivity." The variations in the number of ways that the teaching/learning process may be expected to take place should have a decidedly positive impact on productivity in post-secondary educational institutions. We find the suggestions in the Economic Council's *Seventh Annual Review* on this subject persuasive and worth summarizing. They are as follows:

a) further specialization and coordination among post-secondary institutions, alternation of on-campus instruction with practical work experience, and team teaching with effective use of student assistants:
b) the avoidance of duplication of courses and proliferation of new courses without discarding outmoded courses;
c) the evaluation of costs and benefits of new technologies, services, and building designs;
d) joint operation to get maximum benefit from use of specialized libary and computer facilities.

---

[9] Smith, *op. cit.*, p. 8.
[10] David W. Slater, "Change in the Universities: University Government Relations – Comment I." *Canadian Public Administration*, Spring 1970, Vol. XIII, No. 1., p. 23.

The Review points out that fuller use of facilities in off-peak hours, days, and seasons can be realized by offering people who are already part of the labour force an opportunity to continue their studies on a part-time basis. Many of these points are covered in different sections of the brief; all are important and should be borne in mind.

The post-industrial society is knowledge-based; increased expenditures on education and research therefore should not be a cause of surprise. What we need to establish is the rate of increase which is appropriate. We can anticipate that as the service sectors of the economy increase as a proportion of all economic activity in the post-industrial society there will be greater proportional resources to be allocated through the public sector. Obviously there is a need for planning, for estimating and balancing the various demands. It is wrong to isolate educational costs: they must be viewed within the context of overall social needs.

Professor Dobell has chosen as his examples of trade-offs against increased educational costs those of people's consumption of medical services, food, transport, and environmental improvement. These are obviously "good" alternatives. But to the observer who looks at the luxury that is lavished on new office buildings and apartment blocks, other possible trade-offs will occur. For instance, our society could be allocating more of our wealth for education and less for grand buildings with air-conditioning, broadloom and opulent bathrooms. Perhaps in the world of the future, more and better education – as well as those other "good" alternatives – will be preferable to more and better cars, appliances and boat accessories. Perhaps learning is more productive than advertising or packaging.

Any argument about social goals that calls in question the values and practices of the private sector will be immediately branded by some as "socialist." Galbraith has pointed out that "private virtue still lies, on the whole, in producing more for more money. Public virtue still lies, on the whole, not with the politician who proposes to accomplish more for the same expenditure, but with the one who proposes to do more for less. And the voice of the man who wishes government to do less for less is still heard."[11] The approach taken here to over-all social

[11]Galbraith, *The New Industrial State*, p. 346.

goals is not one that should be identified with a particular form
of government. *Any* government of a modern industrial state
moving rapidly into the post-industrial period will have to take
seriously the priorities that post-industrialism imposes. John P.
Robarts, Prime Minister of the Province of Ontario (1961-
1971) has recognized for some time the new role that government must play in the world of today and tomorrow. Address-
ing the First Provincial-Municipal Conference on April 22nd,
1970, he said:

> During the next decade we shall place less reliance
> on economic growth for its own sake and more on
> the fulfilment of values of society . . . If we are
> going to control our destiny, we must be prepared
> to make certain commitments and accept that there
> will be personal sacrifice for the benefit of society at
> large . . . Governments may have to forbid certain
> types of development to prevent pollution, the de-
> struction of the natural beauty of our countryside or
> the loss of unique landmarks. Industries may not
> always be able to establish on the locations of their
> choice. Housing developments may be prohibited in
> certain areas. There will be stricter controls of eco-
> nomic development.[12]

Galbraith has written of the malaise of North American life
that results from our industrial arrangements, which tend to
choke the individual *qua* consumer with an indigestible plethora of unneeded objects while the individual *qua* citizen lacks
safe and quiet streets, clean water and pure air.[13] For these
essential ingredients of decent living we can look only to governments because the problems of pollution and overcrowding
have already grown beyond the capacity of private individuals
and corporations to cope with, and are worsening daily.

The division of costs between the private and public sectors
in any society at a particular point in time is somewhat fortui-
tous, certainly not sacrosanct. What is important over the com-

---

[12] The Hon. John Robarts, Statement to the First Provincial-Municipal Conference, Toronto, April 22, 1970, pp. 8-10.
[13] J. K. Galbraith, *The Affluent Society* (Boston: Houghton Mifflin, 1958), Ch.
XVIII, and *passim*.

ing decades is to establish the priorities on which planning
must be based. In this process the viewpoint of youth should be
considered as well as the voice of experience, for young people
are the ones who will have to live with the results of present
planning.

Financial Assistance to Students

Several student aid schemes have been proposed which have as
an objective the shifting of a larger portion of the costs of post-
secondary education to the students, by means of the substitution (in varying degrees) of loans for grants. This is the common principle; the particular formulations vary widely.

A fairly extensive literature has grown up around this subject, and therefore we think it superfluous to describe these
proposals in detail or to summarize the reactions to them that
have appeared in various reports. For the Canadian scene, Professor R. M. Pike's wise and meticulous study of the accessibility of higher education in Canada is a landmark in the literature of this area.[14] For Ontario, the report of the CPUO Subcommittee on Student Aid (the Morand Report) is clear and
comprehensive.[15]

Some background information about massive loan-based
schemes is given in an appendix to the Cook-Stager Report.
The first proposal of this kind was made in 1955 by Milton
Friedman; it was kept alive by Seymour Harris, and in 1968 it
was publicized under the name of an Educational Opportunity
Bank (EOB); it has not been implemented anywhere. In Great
Britain, a loan scheme was proposed to the Robbins Commit-
tee on Higher Education in 1963, but was not recommended.

The CPUO Subcommittee on Student Aid studied two proposals based on the EOB idea: the Contingent Repayment Student
Assistance Program (CORSAP) proposed by Cook and Stager,[16]

---

[14] Robert M. Pike, *Who Doesn't Get to University – and Why* (Ottawa: Association of Universities and Colleges of Canada, 1970).
[15] *Undergraduate Student Aid and Accessibility in the Universities of Ontario*,
Report of the Subcommittee on Student Aid to the Committee of Presidents of
Universities of Ontario, 1970.
[16] Cook and Stager, *op. cit.*

and the Council of Ministers' Proposal.[17] The subcommittee's report explains the basic EOB idea:

> As governments find themselves faced in the educational sector with the dilemma of spiralling costs and a commitment to equalize educational opportunity, it has been suggested that under an EOB plan, they could respond by raising the contribution (tuition) expected from students, while at the same time ensuring that anyone who cannot afford this contribution will receive sufficient funds to cover his needs, with the stipulation that some form of repayment is expected at a later time. The amount of repayment would be based on an assessment of benefits the student has received as a result of his post-secondary educational experience, and on his ability to pay. One measure of both criteria could be the graduate's income . . . .

The strongest objections to the EOB idea that are stated in the Morand Report are the following: "the Subcommittee is concerned by the abandon with which proponents of an EOB scheme are prepared to let sixteen-, seventeen- and eighteen-year-olds assume thousands of dollars of debt," and, "an all-loan higher cost EOB scheme would very likely do little to encourage attendance at post-secondary institutions, and . . . the prospects for the universities attracting the children of the lower socio-economic groups would almost certainly be even bleaker."[18]

We are in sympathy with both these objections and support the Morand recommendations that no EOB type concept be introduced in Ontario until much greater certainty has been established about the viability and effects of such a scheme. We would make a further point. The Council of Ministers' proposal is justified on the grounds, *inter alia*, that it gives the lower income groups an opportunity to pay for post-secondary edu-

---

[17] Council of Ministers of Education, Canada: *Summary of Discussions with Representatives of the Federal Government*, Ottawa, 21st April, 1970.
[18] *Undergraduate Student Aid*, pp. 73-74, 77 and 78.

cation by borrowing. The indebtedness could be enormous – so high that it could never be anything resembling an incentive for low income groups; and beyond that, a fundamental ethical principle would be violated. What is unfair about the proposal is that *only the lower income groups would have to accept the penalty of debt.* The proposal expressly states that the student's family still has the responsibility to pay what they can afford. Not all will have to go into debt.

There is a very real cost to being in debt, and it is difficult to see how the principle of equity is served by requiring some to incur debts and others not. Equity is neither served nor denied by conferring a benefit on an individual that he did not previously enjoy. Equity must be determined by examining a person's position relative to others. When the benefit conferred imposes a penalty (fifteen years of indebtedness at prevailing interest rates) which is not required of others who enjoy the same benefit because their parents can afford to help them, this is scarcely equitable. It is a fine-sounding phrase to ask at what stage does the individual "accept his share of responsibility for meeting society's goals", but under this proposal, only the poor would be faced with accepting such responsibility. It is a reactionary social philosophy that would put so many in a debtors' prison at a time in their life cycle when their indebtedness will be increased by mortgages or other expenses connected with establishing themselves in society.

If there is validity in anything that we have said about the need for greater democratization and broader accessibility to post-secondary education in the post-industrial period, then the EOB-type schemes must be characterized as retrograde. A student writes:

> If students in the last half of this decade are going to have to pay more of the share of the cost of their own education, drawing loans of well over $1,000 (and, under some schemes, perhaps as high as $5,-000) for *each year* of their university career, non-vocational education in the humanities is inevitably going to be restricted to children of a privileged sector of the community who can afford to spend three or four years amassing debts of several thousand dollars, without the immediate promise of a

148

highly-paid job following their graduation . . . Perhaps an even graver consideration is that children from low-income families are hardly likely to be encouraged to enter university if it means the accumulation of large-scale debt. In other words, people at the lower end of our economic structure would ostensibly be offered "universal accessibility", but at a price too high to risk; in fact, at a price anywhere from two to ten times higher than at present.[19]

Our own feeling is that there is a great deal to be said for the Province of Ontario Student Awards Program (OSAP). It needs more money and more publicity in the schools, and there are details where improvements could be made, but on the whole it is what the present situation demands – a variable scheme with enormous flexibility.

On the matter of recouping the costs of post-secondary education from those who have been subsidized and have derived great benefits at public expense, we believe that this happens to some extent already through the graduated income tax, and we would argue that this is the proper and appropriate mechanism for such a shift in the impact of costs. Professor R. W. Judy has phrased this very succinctly: "It seems counter-productive . . . to attempt to create greater equality of educational opportunity and income distribution by abolishing tuition fees or instituting student salaries. A better way to achieve these objectives would be to tax more and subsidize less those who are or will be affluent and to subsidize more and tax less those who are poor."[20] Meanwhile we must recognize that, as in so many welfare policies, there is a case for selectivity as opposed to universality, with greater positive discrimination in favour of the disadvantaged.

Some incidental advantages of the use of income tax instead of repayable student aid to recoup the subsidization expenses of post-secondary education are the following: the government

---

[19] Richard Reoch, unpublished letter, August 4, 1970.
[20] R. W. Judy, "On the Income Redistributive Effects of Public Aid to Higher Education in Canada" (Toronto: Institute for the Quantitative Analysis of Social and Economic Policy, University of Toronto, 1969), pp. 26-7.

would recoup these amounts at current price levels and would
not lose out as a result of inflation; the funds would not be
earmarked (and it is said that the receipt of earmarked funds
by governments is a poor principle); and, finally, it seems inappropriate to finance people's schooling on any basis that mar-
ries them to an obligation in one provincial jurisdiction in these
days of increasing mobility. A further consideration is that if
Canada's immigration policies continue to bring in some very
highly qualified immigrants, there would be a sizeable proportion of our work force who would not be carrying the burden
of debt that we would have imposed on the highly-qualified
native-born.

An idea which we propose for consideration is that a student
during his secondary school career should accumulate an entitlement of financial credit towards his post-secondary educational expenses for each period during which he maintains satisfactory standards of achievement; at the time that he is ready
for post-secondary education he would cash in on his credits on
a scale based on his family income. This would be a variation
of the present OSAP scheme, ensuring that at all stages of his
secondary school career, a student would know that the financial possibility of further education existed for him. The standing required to earn these credits must not be placed high,
because then the scheme would be weighted in favour of the
prevailing middle-class values and would fail to motivate the
very under-represented groups. Simply to pass must be sufficient to earn credit.

The purpose of the credit scheme would be to extend the
awareness of post-secondary education to a wider spectrum of
young people, and to introduce the idea to them at an earlier
stage. Properly communicated, the idea of earned credits
should – like the entitlements earned by servicemen in the Second World War – encourage a feeling that post-secondary education is a possibility to be considered. The success of the
veterans' scheme, and the benefits reaped from it ever since,
make us entertain some hopes for the scheme we propose as an
effective weapon in the war against poverty and deprivation.

The problems arising from the cultural deprivation of many
children will not, of course, be solved easily or soon. In the
study referred to earlier, Professor Pike has warned that there
is no easy solution to the problem of the culturally disadvan-

taged child. "Canadian educators . . . are vitally concerned to overcome the lack of motivation, the marked deficiencies in verbal and perceptual development and in the development of abstract concepts of the world (all of which tend to be psychological characteristics of the culturally deprived) through special educational programs designed to develop cognitive skills and motivation for learning amongst disadvantaged young children. It would, however, be naive to expect any quick results from such programs, and extremely naive . . . to expect that, in the near future, greatly increased numbers of hitherto disadvantaged children will gain access to the universities."[21] However, Professor Pike also refutes those who claim that motivation is a greater deterrent than economics and use this argument to justify a laissez-faire approach to problems of inequality of income as they affect the educational opportunities of school children. He points out that the reasons (other than economic) sometimes given for leaving school, such as lack of interest in studies or desire for a job, may well be symptomatic of an interwoven set of family attitudes and circumstances that are inimical to continuing attendance at school and that may well have a root cause that is economic. "In such cases, low income is not necessarily the direct cause of drop-out . . . but nevertheless some kind of positive financial incentive may be required if family members, including the children, are to be convinced that it is worthwhile foregoing immediate earnings from employment in favour of more education, and the financial benefits, in terms of higher earnings at a later date which more education ultimately brings."[22]

A further possibility, already alluded to, would be a "citizens' sabbatical," a periodic study leave made generally available. Something like this seems to follow from the prospect of continuing change, obsolescence of qualifications, a more leisure-oriented society, and the consequent need to extend the period of education. There are many possible ways of financing such a scheme. We have not worked out any details, but we are interested in the idea and put it forward for consideration.

---

[21] Pike, *op. cit.*, p. 86.
[22] *Ibid.*, p. 100.

In summary, then, we would say that a continuation of the very flexible OSAP is best adapted to the immediate future, and we believe that any changes over the years should be made in the direction of means-tested grants for all years of college or university work.

Provincial Revenues and Expenditures on Education

We have referred to the public expressions of concern over the costs of post-secondary education – indeed, of the whole educational establishment. There have been many warnings that a financial apocalypse is fast approaching. Various guesses have been made of the date by which, if recent trends continue, expenditures on education will gobble up the whole of government revenues.

There are patent absurdities in simple statistical extrapolations of total costs which do not take into account the factors which have contributed to those costs and which may not apply in the future. It is true that the growth in the costs of higher education in Ontario was very great in the decade of the sixties. Three principal factors contributed to this growth. First, full-time enrolment in Ontario universities quadrupled during those ten years as a result of substantial increases in both the university-age population and the participation rates. During a relatively short period we had massive growth in numbers of the participating age group coincident with a movement from elitism to more wide-spread participation. In contrast, the projections of full-time enrolment that we believe to be realistic for the seventies show a substantially reduced rate of growth. (Part-time enrolment may be quite another matter.) Second, the sixties saw significant catching-up in sophistication of our universities' libraries and computer systems, and in academic salaries, which had been at relatively low levels. By any standard our academic salary levels are competitive now and we are on the road to consolidation of our systems of libraries and computers. And, third, the accommodation of vastly increased numbers of students required a doubling of the number of universities in Ontario over the decade. In the early years of operation it is characteristic for universities to have high unit costs; as they fill up to capacity, unit costs decrease.

If our suggestions in this brief are found generally acceptable, the need for new institutions will be much less over the next decade than in the last. If, in particular, the new model for the provision of generalist education is adopted, additional places could be provided at somewhat lower operating cost than is possible with expansion on the traditional university model, and, we believe, with no loss of quality, perhaps indeed a gain.

Recent history supports the view that simple extrapolation of costs is inappropriate as a means of foretelling what will happen to costs in the future. There are clear signs of a levelling-off of total provincial expenditures on education in recent years. Educational expenditures (including the primary, secondary and post-secondary levels) consumed about 32 per cent of provincial revenue in 1964-65, increased rapidly over the next three years to about 40 per cent in 1967-68, with the proportion only increasing modestly over the next three years to 41 per cent in 1969-70 and 1970-71. (See Figure 11-1).

In attempting to project the financial outlook, we have taken a look at likely revenues available to the provincial government, and we have then attempted to see what the implications are for funding the anticipated levels of enrolment.

We approach this task with some hesitation because the uncertainties in forecasting income and costs are many. But the attempt must be made for at least two reasons. First, we believe it is appropriate to take a hard look at forecasts of educational costs which have been on the whole generally very gloomy. And second, not to make some estimates of income and costs would invite an onrush of justifiable criticism that we propose some attractive models but completely ignore financing levels that will be required to support these models.

Since reliable forecasts of enrolments in various educational sectors are only available for the period 1971-76 we keep our time horizon for financial analysis limited to that period. The analysis is purposely kept very simple and does not pretend to be an exercise in the application of economic theory to the educational sector. We do offer however a feasible scenario for financing education over the next five years. We would be remiss in our obligations if we did not put forward the best case possible for education. It remains for government to decide, upon the best advice it can get, where education should lie in the system of priorities.

The basis of these financial projections is the set of projections of post-secondary enrolment that have been described and, we think, substantiated, in Chapter four. We reiterate that these projections are based on social demand and continuation of the "open door" policy, and assume no changes in admission requirements. For the primary and secondary levels we have utilized OISE projections.[23]

A major difficulty that we face in projecting government revenues and increases in educational costs is the necessity to make certain assumptions about inflation. In the case of government revenue, the difficulty arises from the "buoyancy" or "fiscal-dividend" aspect of tax revenues. Tax revenues are not a simple function of growth in economic product; under a progressive tax system, tax revenues rise somewhat faster. How much faster they will rise – even in the absence of changes in taxation policy or rates – is not easy to estimate. The existence of this buoyancy, though, means that it is not meaningful to project government revenue in "constant dollars." Thus, projections of income which follow later are in current dollars.

In projecting the effect of inflation on university costs, one faces the problem of choosing an appropriate index. The price of government expenditures as measured by the GNP Implicit Price Index of Government Expenditures on Goods and Services rose at 5½ per cent per year over the decade. In the absence of a specific index of educational costs we feel that this index would be an acceptable proxy for estimating the impact of inflation on the educational sector. We should point out however that some 75 per cent of university budgets goes to salaries, and therefore cost increases will be more closely tied to salary rises than to the price of goods. These difficulties should be kept in mind in considering the analysis that follows.

During the 1960's total provincial revenues increased at an average compound annual rate of nearly 16 per cent, owing in large part to a shift in spending from the private to the public sector. It is probably unrealistic to expect a 16 per cent growth rate to continue through the seventies, but we should point out that the Economic Council of Canada expects a continuing

---

[23] Cicely Watson, *Financing Higher Education, The Next Ten Years,* 1968.

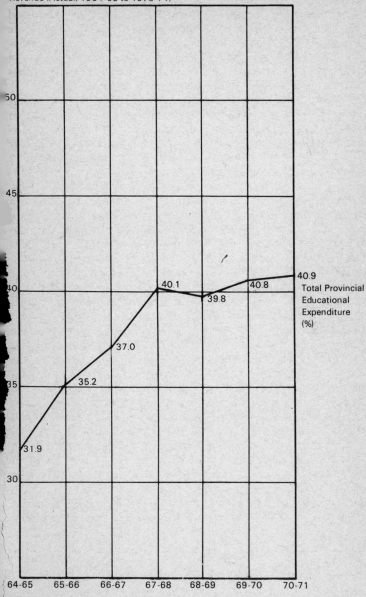

Figure II-I Total Provincial Educational Expenditure as a Percentage of Provincial Revenue (Actual, 1964-65 to 1970-71)

shift in spending from the private to the public sector. Thus, although it is difficult to guess what the magnitude of that shift will be, tax revenues will almost certainly continue to rise faster than growth in the economy. In part, this will result from the "fiscal-dividend" aspect of the progressive tax system. The growth of the Canadian economy (GNP) in recent years has been in the vicinity of 7 per cent per annum; in contrast, provincial government revenue has grown at more than twice that rate primarily due to increased provincial share of personal and corporation taxes and increased transfers from federal government. As we have said earlier maintenance of a high level of federal support underlies our analysis so it seems reasonable to use the 16 per cent rate of increase as an upper bound for the next decade, and half that rate as a lower bound.

Figure 11-2 shows provincial government revenues from 1945 to 1970 plotted with projections to 1980 according to three postulated rates of growth.[24] The upper bound of 16 per cent per annum would approximate the trend of the last 15 years; 8 per cent would represent a considerable departure from the trend. A reasonable expectation might be 12 per cent.

The suggestion that the burden of education costs might be ameliorated by some version of the Educational Opportunity Bank concept has been dealt with earlier. Even if such a scheme were accepted, it would require many years for a steady-state situation to be attained. We trust, however, that the concept will not be invoked on the grounds that we have already given. In any case, as our analysis will show, the future growth in expenditures for education will be substantially less than past rates of growth in educational expenditures. As we indicated above, the rate of increase of educational expenditures as a share of total revenue virtually levelled off from 1967 to 1970. *As one of many possible scenarios for analysis we assume that the share will remain at the level of 41 per cent of provincial revenues.* Government will of course wish to examine other share levels keeping benefits and costs in mind.

In the analysis that we have made of operating costs by educational sector, we have assumed that the relative cost per

---

[24] Historical data for 1945 through 1970 are plotted from Table C9, *Historical Summary of Total Budgetary Transactions*, Ontario Budget 1970, p. 108.

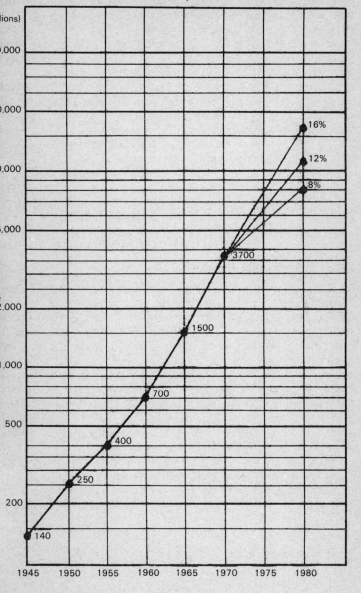

Figure 11-2. Growth of Provincial Net General Revenue (1945 to 1969) and projected from 1970 to 1980 at 8, 12 and 16% per annum.

student of the sectors which obtained in 1968-69 will remain
constant over the period.

Projected Costs to Government

Table H contains historical and projected full-time enrolment
data for the various sectors from 1968-69 to 1975-76. (For the
purposes of this analysis we have omitted the enrolments in
schools of nursing and colleges of agricultural technology; the
minor changes in enrolment that are likely to take place in
these institutions would have only negligible effects on our
results.)

The sector enrolment data for 1968-69 were related to financial data for the same sectors to obtain government support in
operating costs per student by sector. The 1968-69 cost per
student figures were then applied to projected sector enrolments which were then totalled for each of the years 1970-71
through to 1975-76 to yield projections of total costs in 1968-69
dollars for these years (column 2 of Table I).[25]

We have shown on Figure 11-1 the history of net general
revenue of the Province of Ontario with alternative projections
of growth a. ¬ per cent, 12 per cent and 16 per cent through to
1980. It is likely that increasingly buoyant tax revenues for the
period will yield at least 8 per cent annual growth in provincial
revenues and if the trend of the past 15 years were to continue,
growth would approach 16 per cent annually. Growth at a 12
per cent annual rate would thus appear to be a fairly reasonable projection.

For the analysis of projected income to the educational sectors we hold the total share arbitrarily to 41 per cent which was
the approximate level for 1967 to 1970. Column 1 of Table I
shows the projected 41 per cent provincial net general revenue
allocable to education at the alternative growth rate of 8 per
cent, 12 per cent, and 16 per cent. Comparisons of revenue in
current dollars (Column 1) to costs in constant dollars (column
2) at these growth rates are therefore made leaving remainder

---

[25] The financial data were taken from the Public Accounts of the Province of
Ontario for the fiscal year ending March 31, 1969. For detailed calculations see
the original brief presented to the Committee on Post-Secondary Education in
Ontario, January, 1971.

Table H. Sector enrolments 1968-69 through 1975-76

	Year	(1) Primary Enrolment (000)	(2) Secondary Enrolment (000)	(3) Primary & Secondary Enrolment (000)	(4) CAATs (000)	(5) Ryerson (000)	(6) University (000)
Actual	1968-69	1,431.0	504.0	1,935.0	17.8	5.8	103.5
	1969-70	1,456.0	531.0	1,987.0	24.7	5.8	114.0
	1970-71	1,464.0	559.6	2,023.6	34.5	6.4	124.8
Projections	1971-72	1,467.0	584.9	2,051.9	45.8	8.0	137.4
	1972-73	1,455.0	602.6	2,057.6	58.4	9.2	153.0
	1973-74	1,444.0	619.2	2,063.2	71.2	10.1	167.5
	1974-75	1,434.2	623.0	2,057.2	80.0	11.2	186.0
	1975-76	1,429.0	637.6	2,066.6	90.8	12.3	202.7

SOURCE: Primary and secondary enrolments are taken from Cicely Watson, *Financing Higher Education, The Next Ten Years*, 1968. Ryerson Polytechnical Institute supplied the data for that institution. The Department of Education, College of Applied Arts and Technology Branch, Province of Ontario supplied estimates of CAATs enrolments. Projections of universities' enrolments including Teachers' Colleges and OCA are taken from Zsigmond and Wenaas, *Enrolment in Educational Institutions by Province 1951-52 to 1980-81*, 1970.

sums available for inflation, sophistication and development (column 3). The calculations could, of course, be performed for any other assumed share of net general revenue.

It is seen from Table I that, assuming reasonable alternatives of projected revenues, cost increases due to enrolment alone will be relatively modest leaving substantial remainders to take care of the inevitable inflation and to apply to improvements to the system for new developments and sophistication.

The reason that education costs are not projected to grow at the alarming rates projected by some analysts lies in the stabilizing enrolments in primary and secondary schools (see Columns (1) and (2) of Table H). The net effect of these, combined with projected growth rates of enrolment in CAATs and universities, is to redistribute the shares of education resources among the sectors. Table J shows the rather startling shifts in resource allocations resulting from the differential growth rates under the assumptions of this scenario. (We should note also that the primary and secondary enrolment stabilization will have its effect on the postsecondary level in the eighties as students move from one level to the other; the effect will not be so dramatic however because of continuing increases in participation.)

We do *not* believe that the primary and secondary sector shares should be reduced quite so sharply. A portion of the remainder shown in Column (3) of Table I ought to be devoted to improvement in their expenditures per pupil; indeed the Province has a commitment to increase its share of support to 60 per cent, and to relieve the impact of educational costs on rural households.[26] The achievement of equality of educational opportunity which so much concerns us may also depend in part on improvement in the primary and secondary sector. Also, the upgrading of the professional level of primary teachers will have inevitable upward costs effects. On the other hand, we don't see costs per student in the CAATs exceeding those for universities and Ryerson; economies of scale should be realized shortly in these institutions and therefore their costs per student which now approximate those of universities should be reduced.

---

[26] The effect of this would be to redistribute shares of inflated costs so that the extreme reductions implied in Table J for primary and secondary costs in constant dollars would be moderated to some extent.

CHAPTER 12

THE
INTERFACE
WITH
GOVERNMENT

Inevitably the relations of academic institutions and government bodies are sensitive, and they become more so as government provides more, most, now practically all, of the academic institutions' financial support. The relationship has been well described in, for example, the Honourable William G. Davis's Gerstein Lecture. It can result in creative tension, or it can be merely abrasive.

The mechanisms that have been developed in Ontario for handling these sensitive relations – the DUA/CUA/CPUO complex, and the CAAT Branch and Council of Regents – are not an exact copy of anything to be found elsewhere. We shall confine our comments to the former set of arrangements, which are well-established. Those arrangements stand comparison with any jurisdiction. They are open, so that their operation can be understood by any of the public who are interested. They are flexible, and therefore responsive to changing needs. They facilitate close and continuous communication. And the success of their operation can be measured by the response of the system to the not insignificant challenges of the past decade. As well-informed an observer as Professor Robert Berdahl has commented that Ontario has achieved a unique and enviable solution to a universal problem.

We have stressed throughout that the challenges of the decades to come will be great, and also different. What follows are a series of suggested changes in the structures governing the area of our relations with government that we think will be necessary, or at least worth considering, in the years ahead.

1. If post-secondary education in Ontario is to function as an integrated system, the logic of having an integrated government department is compelling, for liaison and planning as well as for administration. We are familiar with the objections to this change. The CAATs, understandably, do not want to be taken over or swallowed up – they want to develop their ethos in their own way. And the universities want to preserve their standards, their emphasis on excellence, their concern for the advancement of knowledge and wisdom, so as to remain worthy citizens among the universities of the world. The universities are afraid that their own distinctive problems would be lost sight of, or, indeed, that their very nature would be compromised, if they were thrown in with the other new, faster-growing sector of post-secondary education.

   On the other hand, the disadvantages of continued rivalry are serious: two groups whose co-ordination and mutual assistance are vital for the future would continue to be competitors for the resources made available to post-secondary education, and the principles of democratization and flexibility would be frustrated by the rigid barrier that exists at present. We believe that it is in the public interest for the whole post-secondary field to be more closely related than it is. There may well be very little substance to the fears that are expressed, provided that the universities and the CAATS maintain their separate committees of presidents to formulate and to advocate their distinctive needs.

2. We would visualize a Minister of Post-Secondary Education having the responsibilities of the present Minister of University Affairs for the fourteen provincially-assisted universities; certain scientific and cultural entities (Royal Ontario Museum, Royal Botanical Gardens, Ontario Col-

lege of Art, Ontario Research Foundation); for the Colleges of Applied Arts and Technology; for Ryerson (whether Polytechnical Institute or fifteenth university); and also for whatever body is developed (if any) to meet future needs along the lines of our suggested University of Ontario, the sixteenth university. He would, of course, have to ensure effective liaison between his department and those of Education, Agriculture, Health, and other departments with direct interests in post-secondary education. In addition it would be crucially important for him to work closely with whatever minister and/or agency of the Federal Government was responsible for the federal involvement in post-secondary education in the future. At the very least this would be a federal Minister of Science; but we would hope that during the next ten or fifteen years the Government of Canada will be persuaded to take a much more active part in post-secondary developments along one of the lines we have suggested.

3. The intermediary – the Committee on University Affairs – would become the Committee on Post-Secondary Affairs and would include laymen and academics with close connections with the CAATs. The CUA has worked well with its present personnel; unlike many advisory bodies it has not been merely a "front" – there has been, through it, real academic influence on policy. As the future unfolds we think there should be consideration of developing an arrangement that would have firmer safeguards for the academic voice, rather than depending on the goodwill of particular individuals. Such an arrangement could be achieved by providing for more academic representation (which will be necessary in any case if the colleges are to be part of the same system), by having more than one full-time member, and by giving the Committee a secretariat independent of the government department. The departmental connection of the present CUA has undoubtedly expedited its work, but it has also influenced its thinking towards the Treasury Board's way of looking at things. It could be argued that one Treasury Board is enough, and that somewhere in the system a group should be seriously asking, not only: "Is x per cent of the GPP too much for post-secondary education?" but also: Is x per cent *sufficient*?"

With the gradual devolution of certain powers to regional centres in the province, it will be advisable to consider the setting up of regional advisory boards to the Committee on Post-Secondary Education. Such boards would be helpful in dealing with exclusively regional concerns, and could advise about local circumstances, for example, educational needs of Canada's native peoples, or specific developments in the industrial picture, or services to predominantly French-speaking communities. In sparsely-populated parts of the province it will be necessary to coordinate resources and improve communications a great deal in order to achieve real equality of opportunity.

It is worth recalling that when the four newest Ontario universities – Trent, Brock, Lakehead and Laurentian – were in process of being established, the Province of Ontario was committed not only to the "open door" policy but also to the assumption that a substantial number of undergraduate places should be provided away from major metropolitan areas of the province. These institutions would bring opportunity closer to many young people in the province, thus contributing to equality of opportunity. Also, these were all established as independent universities rather than liberal arts colleges affiliated with existing institutions; this decision implied that they were of equal status and should aspire to a quality comparable to that of existing institutions. That was a generous decision, reflecting a concept of what was due to the young people of Ontario (especially those in isolated regions) in which we should take pride. In these circumstances it would be wrong for any of these institutions to aspire, or to be told to aspire, to anything less than equivalent academic opportunities for its students – certainly in generalist and specialist undergraduate education, even if constraints have to be recognized as inevitable in advanced and professional courses. Yet the obstacles to achieving even this limited goal are formidable

The special problems of the two northern universities in Ontario are additional to the normal problems associated with "emergence"; their solution requires purposeful action by the institutions themselves, by sister institutions and by government; and action by government may well involve the deliberate recognition of a role for these institutions, in the regions where they are located, that goes well beyond the responsibilities of universities in the wealthier and more populous areas. Universities in the north should be supported as a species of tertiary industry, as well as for other reasons. The same considerations apply to northern colleges.

We mention this problem simply to reinforce our hope that regional considerations will somehow be permitted to emerge, forcefully, in whatever structure is developed.

4. The Committee of Presidents of Universities of Ontario – augmented, presumably, in the course of time, by presidents and colleagues from Ryerson and the University of Ontario – would continue as a distinct body to function as the chief spokesman for the universities. We would also expect that the organization of CAAT Presidents will continue to represent their special interests, and it is obvious that much closer liaison will develop between the two bodies.

As we have indicated earlier in the brief, some substantial steps have already been taken to modify university autonomy in the general interest. This will continue. CPUO will continue to develop techniques of rationalization and coordination, as we have done over the years, gradually working out mechanisms that serve the best interests of the Province and at the same time preserve the values of institutional autonomy.

EPILOGUE

We have tried throughout to take the long-term view, and we have deliberately chosen a view as optimistic as we honestly could. Often the future is painted in darker hues. We believe, however, that given half a chance man's goodness and ingenuity will prove to be equal to the formidable difficulties ahead.

We have emphasized the various *implications* of the long-term view: the speed of change, the new ways of looking at profit, employment and certification, the greater dependence on complex theoretical knowledge (and the resulting importance of handling such knowledge), the shifting balance of work and leisure (and the resulting opportunities for cultural enrichment and enjoyment), and the responsibility to use the vast potential of scientific and technological resources to improve human life and solve local, provincial, national and global problems.

We have adopted *accessibility* of post-secondary education as the major principle that should govern future developments. This has always been a matter of abstract justice, more recently of social right, and with the new centrality of knowledge it will

become a matter of necessity. We have shown that this is going
to involve a greater geographic and socio-economic outreach
than before, and (eventually) an extension of the "open door"
policy to the highest levels. With the existing (well documented)
class structure of Canada and the way in which the dice are
loaded against the children of the poor, we have examined
what the post-secondary educational part of the social milieu
can do to redress the balance, and we believe it can do a great
deal. We suggest ways of broadening the base and opening and
multiplying the upward routes of the system of post-secondary
education so that no student will find himself blocked from
further progress by rigidities in the system. We have urged
special concern for young people in isolated and sparsely popu-
lated parts of the province. Regarding the financial support of
students, we hope to see a progressive development from the
present loan/grant arrangement to a greater proportional reliance on grants (subject to means tests), and we have suggested
that financial credits towards post-secondary educational expenses might be accumulated by students during their years in
secondary school. We visualize a multiplication of opportunities for post-secondary education across the province, and have
suggested an investigation of one particular method that has an
interesting potential for quality and economy.

We believe that education is becoming a *lifetime* matter, to
be continued or resumed at intervals in order to keep up with
the pace of change; certification or licensure will become a
periodic necessity, with a concomitant need for the "re-tool-
ing" of professional workers, including university professors
and possibly extending to most workers in society. This involves an increasing interpenetration of the worlds of work and
of education and is the basis of two suggestions: a system of
"citizens' sabbaticals," and the recognition of units of work
experience in lieu of formal educational prerequisites where this
is appropriate.

We have stressed the *national* importance of post-secondary
education – as a unifying force within the country to foster a
truly Canadian English-speaking and French-speaking civilization and culture, a means of repaying our educational indebtedness abroad and assisting underdeveloped nations, and an
area where Canada's contribution could be outstanding. With
this in mind we have dealt briefly with Canadian science policy

and have examined at some length the role of the federal government in post-secondary education and the constitutional issues involved.

Viewing post-secondary education as a *provincial* concern, we have tried to make a case for a system that would be better integrated (e.g. through the "University of Ontario" concept for bringing the Colleges of Applied Arts and Technology into a well-defined relationship with the universities characterized by flexibility and vertical mobility for the students), and at the same time more decentralized, based upon the existing regional development areas where appropriate. A corollary is a single Department of Post-Secondary Affairs, and probably a single advisory body. We have looked at the capacity of the existing institutions, the expected enrolments, the gap that will develop soon even if only full-time enrolments are considered, and the costs of education as a proportion of provincial expenditures, now and in the future.

Again, in relation to the *quality of life*, we have given repeated emphasis to flexibility and ready response to change. We question whether over-specialization rather than over-production is the problem of graduate schools and suggest a "troika" variation in the traditional pattern of the Ph.D. We expect the interdisciplinary approaches to learning and research to increase and the organizational bases of such approaches to be shifting and resilient. The life-style of academic workers in the future is likely to be less stereotyped since there will be different roles within the academic profession filling different needs, for example, professor-researcher, professor-teacher, professor-tutor. We have suggested that since tenure is becoming anomalous it should be replaced by agreements carefully devised so as to preserve, amongst other things, the freedom of dissent. We have described the radical and non-radical views of the academic community (which seem likely to co-exist for some time), and the radically different expectations that the students of the future have as compared with those of the past, and we suggested that their emphasis on the wholeness of experience should be admissible in the "house of intellect." We have raised, though not pursued, the question whether a system of post-secondary education geared to a capitalist economy would be valid in either a welfare state or a socialist society.

Finally, though we have spoken much of change, our concern for continuity is manifest in our attempts to ensure that the timeless tasks – preserving knowledge, teaching/learning, research and criticism – will still be performed, and well performed, in Ontario.

REFERENCES

BELL, DANIEL, "The Measurement of Knowledge and Technology" in E.B. Sheldon and W.E. Moore, eds., *Indicators of Social Change*, New York: Russell Sage, 1968.

BELL, DANIEL, "Notes on the Post-Industrial Society," *The Public Interest*, Winter 1967 and Spring 1967.

BEN-DAVID, JOSEPH, *Fundamental Research and the Universities*, Paris: OECD, 1968.

BIRNBAUM, N., "Is There a Post-Industrial Revolution?," *Social Policy*, Vol. 1, No. 2, July-August 1970.

COMMISSION ON THE FINANCING OF HIGHER EDUCATION (V.W. Bladen, chairman), *Financing Higher Education in Canada*, Ottawa: Association of Universities and Colleges of Canada, 1965.

COMMISSION ON THE GOVERNMENT OF THE UNIVERSITY OF TORONTO, *Towards Community in University Government*, Toronto: University of Toronto Press, 1970.

COMMITTEE ON AIMS AND OBJECTIVES OF EDUCATION IN THE SCHOOLS OF ONTARIO (E. M. Hall and L. Dennis, Chairmen), *Living and Learning*, Toronto: Dept. of Education, 1968.

COMMITTEE OF PRESIDENTS OF UNIVERSITIES OF ONTARIO, *Post-Secondary Education in Ontario, 1962-1970*, Toronto: C.P.U.O., 1963.

COOK, G.A. and D.A.A. STAGER, *Student Financial Assistance Programs*, Toronto: Institute for the Quantitative Analysis of Social and Economic Policy, University of Toronto, 1969.

CORRY, J.A., *Farewell the Ivory Tower: Universities in Transition*, Montreal: McGill-Queen's University Press, 1970.

DOMINION BUREAU OF STATISTICS, *Survey of Higher Education Part I: Fall Enrolment in Universities and Colleges*, 1965-66 and 1969-70.

DUFF, SIR JAMES and R.O. BERDAHL, *University Government in Canada*, Toronto: University of Toronto Press, 1966.

ECONOMIC COUNCIL OF CANADA, *Patterns of Growth* (Seventh Annual Review), Ottawa: Queen's Printer, 1970.

ECONOMIC COUNCIL OF CANADA, *Perspective 1975* (Sixth Annual Review), Ottawa: Queen's Printer, 1969.

FROMM, E., *The Revolution of Hope*, New York: Bantam Books, 1968.

GALBRAITH, J.K., *The Affluent Society*, Boston: Houghton Mifflin, 1958.

GALBRAITH, J.K., *The New Industrial State*, Boston: Houghton Mifflin, 1967.

GLASS, J.R., "Equality, Quantity and Quality in Education," *OECD Observer*, June 1969.

GROSS, BERTRAM, *The State of the Nation: Social Systems Accounting*, London: Tavistock, 1966.

HARRIS, ROBIN, *Quiet Evolution: a Study of the Ontario Educational System*, Toronto: University of Toronto Press, 1967.

HURTUBISE, R. and D.C. ROWAT, *The University, Society and Government*, Ottawa: University of Ottawa Press, 1970.

JUDY, R.W., "On the Income Redistributive Effects of Public Aid to Higher Education in Canada," Toronto: Institute for the Quantitative Analysis of Social and Economic Policy, University of Toronto, 1969. Mimeographed.

KAHN, H. and A.J. WIENER, *The Year 2000*, New York: Macmillan, 1967.

LAING, R.D., *The Politics of Experience*, London: Penguin Books, 1967.

LAMONTAGNE, M., *et al.*, *A Science Policy for Canada*, Vol. I. Ottawa: Queen's Printer, 1970.

LAPP, P.A. *et al.*, *Ring of Iron: a Study of Engineering Education in Ontario*, Toronto: C.P.U.O., 1970.

LASKIN, BORA, *Canadian Constitutional Law*, Toronto: Carswell Co. Ltd., 1959.

LASKIN, BORA, *et al.*, *Graduate Studies in the University of Toronto: Report of the President's Committee on the School of Graduate Studies*, Toronto: University of Toronto Press, 1965.

LAW, HARRIET, "Strong Medicine for Scientists Facing a Plethora of Ph.D.'s,"*Canadian University & College*, Vol. 5, No. 10, Oct. 1970.

MACDONALD, J.B., *et al.*, *The Role of the Federal Government in Support of Research in Canadian Universities*, Ottawa: Queen's Printer, 1968.

MACLEISH, ARCHIBALD, "The Revolt of the Diminished Man," *Saturday Review of Literature*, June 7, 1969.

MACPHERSON, B., *et al.*, *Report of the Presidential Advisory Committee on Undergraduate Instruction in the Faculty of Arts and Science, University of Toronto*, Toronto: University of Toronto Press, 1967.

MCLUHAN, H.M., *The Medium is the Massage*, New York: Bantam Books, 1967.

MCPHERSON, HUGO, "The Future of Literary Studies and the Media," *Transactions of the Royal Society of Canada*, Series IV, Vol. VII, 1969.

MEAD, MARGARET, *Culture and Commitment: A Study of Generation Gap*, Garden City, N.Y.: Doubleday & Co., 1970.

MORAND, P., *et al.*, *Undergraduate Student Aid and Accessibility in the Universities of Ontario: Report of the Subcommittee on Student Aid*, Toronto: C.P.U.O., 1970.

PIKE, R.M., *Who Doesn't Get to University – and Why*, Ottawa: Association of Universities and Colleges of Canada, 1970.

PORTER, JOHN, "Post-Industrialism, Post-Nationalism and Post-Secondary Education," *Canadian Public Administration*, Vol. XIV, No. 1, Spring 1971.

ROYAL COMMISSION ON DOMINION-PROVINCIAL RELATIONS, *Report*, Ottawa: King's Printer, 1940.

ROYAL COMMISSION OF INQUIRY IN EDUCATION IN THE PROVINCE OF QUEBEC, *Report*, Quebec: Queen's Printer, 1963-66.

ROYAL COMMISSION ON NATIONAL DEVELOPMENT IN THE ARTS, LETTERS AND SCIENCES, *Report*, Ottawa: King's Printer, 1951.

SLATER, D.W., "Change in the Universities: University Government Relations – Comment I," *Canadian Public Administration*, Vol. XIII, No. 1, Spring, 1970.

SPINKS, J.W.T., *et al.*, *Report of the Commission to Study the Development of Graduate Programs in Ontario Universities*, Toronto: University of Toronto Press, 1966.

TANNER, J.M., *Growth at Adolescence*, Oxford: Blackwell Scientific Publications, 1962.

TRUDEAU, P.E., *Federalism and the French Canadians*, Toronto: Macmillan, 1968.

WATSON, C., *Financing Higher Education, The Next Ten Years*, Toronto: Ontario Institute for Studies in Education, 1968.

WATSON, C. AND S. QUAZI, *Ontario University and College Enrolment Projections to 1981-82* (1968 projection), Enrolment Projection Series No. 4., Toronto: Ontario Institute for Studies in Education, 1968.

ZSIGMOND, Z.E. AND C.J. WENAAS, *Enrolment in Educational Institutions by Province, 1951-52 to 1980-81*, Staff Study No. 25, prepared for the Economic Council of Canada, Ottawa: Economic Council, 1970.